Take Me Home to Afrika

Take Me Home to Afrika

An Autobiography of a Returnee

JOANN MERRITT SCHOFIELD-CHILDS

iUniverse, Inc.
Bloomington

TAKE ME HOME TO AFRIKA
AN AUTOBIOGRAPHY OF A RETURNEE

iUniverse books may be ordered through booksellers or by contacting:

iUniverse
1663 Liberty Drive
Bloomington, IN 47403
www.iuniverse.com
1-800-Authors (1-800-288-4677)

ISBN: 978-1-4620-3699-8 (sc)
ISBN: 978-1-4620-3701-8 (hc)
ISBN: 978-1-4620-3700-1 (ebk)

Printed in the United States of America

iUniverse rev. date: 09/26/2011

Contents

Dedication vii

Acknowledgements...ix

Foreword...xi

Preface..xiii

Introduction..xv

Chapter 1   Listening to Spirit.....................................1

Chapter 2   I Grew Up Knowing Something Was Not
             Right About Being An Afrikan In America..................5

Chapter 3   God's Trying To Tell You Something...........................8

Chapter 4   What Would You Go Back To Afrika For?..................10

Chapter 5   It's A Boy!..13

Chapter 6   Love At First Sight!....................................16

Chapter 7   Life Goes On..19

Chapter 8   Back In Love Again! 23

Chapter 9   Take Me To Afrika And Let's Get Married!..............29

Chapter 10   Did We Miss God?....................................32

Chapter 11   A Blessing In Disguise 37

Chapter 12   Bye-Bye, America 44

Chapter 13   Dear Ancestors We Are Home...........................50

Chapter 14   Checking Out Accra, The Capital 54

Chapter 15   Why Don't You Come To Cape Coast?..................57

Chapter 16   Settling Down In Aquarium Down 62

Chapter 17   Handling Our Business 69

Chapter 18   Where Else Can An Afrikan Call Home?.................75

Chapter 19   "A Bad Day In Ghana Is Better Than
              A Good Day In The Usa"(Unknown).........................78

Chapter 20   Buying Land In Ghana, Class 101.............................81

Chapter 21   If At First You Don't Succeed, Try Again 87

Chapter 22   Down And Out In Ghana......................................91

Chapter 23   Three Little Words-Please Forgive Us.......................95

Chapter 24   Home Sweet Home..98

Chapter 25   Let There Be Light 102

Chapter 26   Alien Resident In The Land Of
              My Ancestral Roots 105

Chapter 27   Honorable House Of Chiefs................................110

Chapter 28   Thank You For Our Inheritance!.........................113

Chapter 29   Kofi Are You Leaving Me?.................................117

Chapter 30   A Traditional Ghanaian Home Going 123

Chapter 31   Fortieth Day Ceremony-One Year
              Memorial For Kofi..134

Chapter 32   President And Mrs.Obama Welcome To Ghana! 138

Chapter 33   Let Go And Let Ghana......................................141

Chapter 34   Where Is The Authentic Afrikan? 159

Chapter 35   Thin Line Between Family And Friend 162

Chapter 36   We Are Family..167

Chapter 37   On My Own 180

Dedication

To Our Ancestors, those who are with us that we cannot see, especially to my parents Mr. Willie Joe Merritt, Mrs. Ruth M. Gunn Merritt and my sister Sylvia Merritt Plummer, the angel who enabled me to meet my soul mate.

To my one and only son, Latif Merritt Schofield; he is the keeper of my dreams.

Last but not the least, In Loving Memory of my Dear Kofi, your name is forever written across my heart. You were certainly an angel appointed to me from the Most High! Without you there would be no story to tell, all because you loved me.

There is only one life
That life is Gods life
That life is perfect
That life is my life
Now!
Ernest Holmes

Acknowledgements

I sincerely thank Mrs. Anastasia Hooper for her editing assistance. She read and re-read this manuscript and gave helpful comments from the Ghanaian perspective. Aunt Fannie Clark during her critique unknowingly gave me a chapter title. My dear Queen E. Malkia Brantuo now of blessed memory offered invaluable advice and corrections. Mr. Albie and Mrs. Rose Walls were constructive with proofreading enabling me to rewrite the manuscript. Professor G.S. Ayernor, President of the Afrikan Renaissance Foundation served as my content editor assisting me with yet another rewrite. Ultimately, my confidant, sister, and friend Professor Nancy Fairley pressed me to delve deeper than I believed I could-to write even more and condense the chapters. A counsel of seven is better than one going it alone. I appreciate all of your forthrightness, encouragement and support enabling me to bring this book to a successful end. May the good you do always come back to you. I am grateful to the Supreme Intelligence that flowed through us all.

Foreword

This book chronicles an amazing journey to the Motherland by Adjoa Childs and her beloved husband Kofi Childs. In July of 1999, Adjoa and Kofi, left family and friends in Philadelphia and moved permanently to Ghana. Finally their lifelong dream became a reality—they were going to live in an "African World". As a Fulbright scholar, I arrived in Ghana in September of the same year. Within a month I meet Adjoa and Kofi at Zion House, the family home of the Amos-Abanyie family. In fact, all three of us, at different times, were officially adopted into this family!

As an anthropologist I am familiar with the literature on the acclimation of repatriates in African nations. Once their romantic ideas about Africa are shattered by reality many repatriates struggle and some even return to the West. In the twenty years I have been teaching, researching and vacationing in Ghana, I have seen malcontented repatriates whose love of the land remain unshakeable as their disdain for the inhabitants grew. Prior to visiting Ghana, Adjoa and Kofi had romanticized their "Motherland"; however, once they faced the daily realities of Ghanaian life they did not retreat in anger or become indifferent. Instead they became more resourceful, flexible and pragmatic. Adjoa and Kofi embraced elements of the local culture which enriched their lives and they accepted that there are 'some things Ghanaian' which they will never understand. But one thing they learned after a decade is that Ghanaians are nothing more and nothing less than humans!

In the pages that follow the reader will come to admire Adjoa for sharing some many of the intimate details of her life in Ghana! We see her grow spiritually, emotionally, socially and intellectually. This autobiography is a love story between two mature adults. It is a spiritual awakening for Adjoa who learns to trust the God within! It is an inspirational account of faith in the goodness of humanity! It is an identity narrative about discovering what it means to be African. Lastly, it is a coming of age tale – in Ghana Adjoa learned to embrace her own agency as a woman of African descent!

Preface

It is my hope that every man, woman, boy and girl who read's this book would gain the courage and faith to move towards whatever dream is deposited within your own spirit. If you have a dream consider yourself fortunate because it means God has given you the dream and God is the means through which your dream will be manifested. God in you is your confidence for success.

This story is written as a tribute to my husband John Calvin Kofi Childs. By writing this story I was able to channel the grief that overcame me after he made his transition and joined the ancestors 9th February, 2009 in Ghana, West Afrika. We experienced a real love at first sight relationship which grew and formed a foundation for an everlasting friendship resulting in marriage until death parted us. I want to testify of his vision, his tenacity, and the adventures we shared after making the decision to move from the United States and return to our motherland Afrika in July of 1999.

We courageously said to each other let's go home to Afrika! We put our faith in God and chose Ghana as our destination. We didn't know anyone in Ghana and we never visited the continent before but we had a burning desire to connect with our Afrikan heritage.

The nine and half years we spent together in Ghana were full of ups and downs yet were filled with contentment. It took more than our social work backgrounds to prepare us for the new life ahead of us. It took all of our love and passion for Afrika along with our commitment to each other, with a pioneering spirit in order to make the connection but most importantly it took the grace of Almighty God.

I write as a legacy for my family, and pray it strengthens the bond between us, helps them to understand me better and the choices I've made. We are family no matter what, no matter where we are; there is no separation in the spiritual sense because with love I always and at all times want Gods' best for each and every one of them.

At the same time I write this story to serve as a roadmap for many who are considering visiting or repatriation to the continent of Afrika, Ghana West Afrika specifically.

More importantly I need to testify how faithful the Lord has been and continues to be in my life.

Introduction

This is my story, and no one can tell it but me. I write of the journey called life. It's about living, loving, searching for meaning and seeking a relationship with God in a real and personal way. I wanted to write about some of my experiences to document how our Creator loves us so much and wants to give us the desires of our heart.

Whatever we consistently desire, imagine, and pursue can be ours! By trusting God I have proven this to myself in my own small way. It's good we don't all want the same things. So whatever it is you're longing for, all I ask you to do is put working clothes on your faith and go for it! When you step out into the unknown, when you jump off the cliff; God is there to catch you and you will soar.

I didn't want anything grand like mansions, riches, yachts or diamonds. I yearned for my homeland Afrika, to live there in a house with an ocean view and I wanted to be there with John the man I loved. This is a story about dreams coming true and this is a love story.

My husband and I experienced a real love at first sight relationship which ended due to the fact he was married. Yet fate brought us together again more than ten years later after he divorced. We had the mutual desire to repatriate to Afrika and this story is about the joys and challenges of the walk of faith adventure. We married, loved and lived nine and a half years together in Ghana until John made his transition to be with the Ancestors.

The two of us longed for Afrika since our childhood and answered the Spirit's call to return to the continent of our heritage. We found our destiny and our inheritance by returning home to the land of our roots. It took the grace of Almighty God and our love for each other and for Afrika to see us through the reconnecting process.

I will not say the faith walk was easy, it was not. Many times I felt I had been forsaken and abandoned but that was never true. Thankfully those times were fleeting and I did not linger long at the pity parties.

I looked at past victories since childhood while my faith grew through overcoming challenges as God was by my side. I was consistently learning that the Most High God would never leave me nor forsake me..

As for me I found out all the songs of faith are true, the Holy Scriptures, the messages of positive thinking, the common thread running through religions is: God loves us and wants the best for us!

The moral of this story can be applied to many circumstances in which one may find them self wanting to pursue a desire that requires moving forward in active faith. As it is said, "the journey of a thousand miles begins with a single step."

It is in taking the initial step, that leap of faith I found myself in a whole new world, a world of possibilities. It seemed the whole universe opened up to escort me, to befriend me and support me along my new faith journey; and I travelled out of this material world into the spiritual one. I had the "Presence" to guide me, provide for me; to defend me and to be the source of all that I needed for a successful life.

I found signposts showing me to turn this way or that way but they were not visible street signs, these signs were divinely revealed. Some things you just know that you know but can't explain how you know them; they're just spiritually discerned. I learned to see with my inner eye and hear with my inner ear.

Also God uses people to bring about his will in our lives. He uses you and he uses me. There are people who obey the promptings of the Holy Spirit to do the right thing at the right time and do good deeds for "goodness sake" alone. In my life I call these people angels. When I speak of angels I give this title to persons God uses in a positive manner to guide us, counsel us and assist us along life's excursion. The Bible says that we often entertain angels unaware. There have been many in my life and I appreciate them all! There were a couple of times when strangers helped us and when we turned to thank them they vanished. I'm certain that you can look back and see angels in your own life too, some of them you know personally and some you don't know.

In 1Cor.2:9 KJV it says eye has not seen nor ear heard, neither have entered the heart of man, the things which God has prepared for them that love him. My life is a testimony to this truth!

Some of the names in this story are real and some have been changed to protect the privacy of individuals, businesses, the innocent and the guilty. It is never my intention to offend anyone as I describe my experiences while I aim to offer non-judge mental observations. I ask forgiveness if I offend unintentionally.

When I speak of an African as a Black person I want to capitalize it. Also I will spell Afrika for Africa and Afrikan to replace African. As the writer of this story I reserve the poetic license to define myself, my race and my continent from an Afro-centric ethos.

Please don't' get hung up on the name or title God because I'll use it a lot. We all know that we ourselves did not create the universe with its untold number of galaxies. We do not give ourselves the breath that we breathe. There is someone, some power greater in control, please find the name and title that brings your salvation. I've found the sooner we acquiesce and cooperate with the Divine One, The Christ, Creator of the universe the better our lives will be.

"If you don't understand yourself
You don't understand anybody else"
Nikki Giovanni

1

Listening to Spirit

My parents Mr. Willie Joe and Mrs. Ruth Merritt named me Joann after my father. We lived in South Philadelphia until I was four years old and I was an only child. We resided on the second floor of an apartment building where all who stayed there were friendly as family. I remember being treated like a princess by my parents and all the neighbors. I went from house to house visiting, feeling very cared for and safe in my all Black community. My family attended Wesley Methodist Church. I remember enjoying the children's classes and being the flower girl in a couple of weddings.

Too many children of today missed out on the era of the close knit family and community; when the whole neighborhood "village" raised a child. During my childhood the adults kept watch over all the kids in the neighborhood and reported all misbehavior. I was chastised by neighbors and given words of wisdom if mom wasn't present, and when mom heard of any wrong doing I was punished by her also. The young ones were kept on the straight and narrow and taught to respect themselves and others. I remember the good feeling of being loved and protected by everyone I knew. Today we have strayed too far from our cooperative communal ways and have suffered for it as an Afrikan family as a whole.

I felt uprooted at the age of four when my parents and I moved to North Philadelphia. My parents had a vision to be upwardly mobile and we now lived in our own private row house on a lovely tree-lined street with a mixed ethnic population. My mother was a housewife and my father worked in building construction.

I remember my father taking me to work with him once or twice. We rode two underground trolleys' to the suburbs where there were no Black people in sight but my father's co-workers. Dad placed me in a corner and gave me a piece of wood block and a toy hammer and I thought I was working alongside him as he was building houses.

Life in this new neighborhood gave me my first interaction to play with Caucasian children. I didn't know I was different until then. These were the only children to play with at the time. The Black couples didn't have any children.

Although I had a good foundation of positive self esteem I was taken aback by being called names that I didn't know the meaning of and never heard before. Yet I knew by the tone they were said, that they weren't nice things to say. I wasn't used to people wanting to touch my hair and ask me why it was the texture it was or ask me why was my skin so dark? These were different experiences for me and confusing; I hadn't even started school yet.

Once, my mom allowed me to invite one "white" girl to our house for lunch. I walked the girl home and waited outside her house and I overheard her father fuss at her for going into my house. When she later came out to play she screamed about how she became sick and up-chucked all the food she had eaten at our house. My mom prepared Campbell chicken noodle soup and a cheese sandwich and I didn't get sick.

On our street lived a nice elderly Caucasian couple who didn't have any children. Mr. and Mrs. Clark whom I liked and I spent some afternoons with them rather than with the disagreeable kids on the block. I would go all around the neighborhood with them as they walked their dog named King. They told me that those children didn't have any manners.

Gradually, more Afrikan families moved into the neighborhood with children and I soon had a host of amicable friends. The Hodges Family, who now live in Washington D.C. and the Bell's have been my friends ever since this young age. Needless to say all the Caucasians eventually moved out of the neighborhood.

So you see I had an early introduction to race relations in America before I'd entered kindergarten. I went to school at the age of four because I turned five in the month of October. What do children know about racism except for what their parents teach them? My parents taught me to respect myself and others, to treat people the way I wanted to be treated and to forgive others because many times people don't know why they do the things they do.

A year later upon my return home from school one afternoon I was surprised with a little baby sister. Mom and dad didn't prepare me well for her arrival. I was supposed to be happy but I wasn't because all of a sudden I was not the star and I was no longer the center of attention. I enjoyed having my mom and dad to myself.

My sister Sylvia was born six years after me and I held it against her well into my late teens I'm ashamed to say. I think it was because everywhere I went I always had to drag her along at my mother's demand. Who wants to have to take their little sister to parties with them or have them tag along to their girlfriends house and she was a tattle-tale too. By the time my sisters Renee and Valerie were born I became less selfish regarding having siblings and welcomed them into the family and we all got along well through the years.

I remember crying so much the first night my mom went to work. I was so used to her being at home preparing a nice hot breakfast for me before school and she was home to greet me for lunch and upon my return from school at the end of the day. It was a difficult adjustment for me when she took on the position as a companion to a family during the night shift.

Dad's work was as a lather building houses was seasonal and in many winters there was no work for him on the construction sites so mom took up the slack and became the breadwinner for the family. But if we were poor I didn't know it. My parents thoroughly invested in bringing up their children the best they could. So dad became the stay at home father and they practiced role reversals out of necessity before it became fashionable as in recent times. This is when I had to become the big sis and the mom when mom was not at home.

My dad was a jovial man, very sociable and I got my work ethic from him because he was never late and rarely out sick from work. My mom was the disciplinarian and a very charitable person to those in need. She taught all of us how to read and write before we went to school. They were not affectionately demonstrative in their love for us but we knew we were loved because they provided well for us. After school we had quality family time where we were helped with our lessons, we played together and were taught to pray. We talked about current events and they taught us values which built good character and prepared us for life.

I remember the times when we went to church as a family but this time we joined a Baptist church and later our parents wouldn't attend but send us to church. We participated in vacation Bible school and my sisters were allowed to go summer Christian camps which I never did. They had a chance to get out of the inner city to the wide open spaces and fresh air of the country side. My sister Renee told me a funny story of when they asked her if she wanted to accept Jesus as her personal savior-she told them she didn't know, she'd have to ask her parents first. A couple of times my sisters and I went in the front door of the church and out the side door and ran to spend our offering money at the candy store. Naughty girls!

Truly though I can say I was sensitive to the voice of Spirit as a child. Once at age five or six I was carrying home a dozen boxes of cookies sold as a fundraiser for the school; the voice said to me don't go that way, go this way. I obeyed and saw two big boys crouched down behind a car waiting for me to pass by. I'm sure they had plans to snatch my parcel from me but I was able to run away from them fast before they could see I changed directions. There was another time I used to take a short cut and walk through an alley but on one certain day; Spirit said "don't go that way today." I obeyed and when I reached the other end of that place there was a pervert in the alley exposing his-self.

I have numerous stories of this nature. There was another time my dad fell asleep watching television while smoking. Spirit woke me up and told me to go downstairs to awaken my father; the couch was burning once I got there. My mother was at work and my sisters were in bed sleeping.

I knew the voice of God early in life ever before I understood what Jesus, sin, salvation and repentance was all about. I knew the Spirit of the living God and He / She knew me too, sometimes the voice was of a female. Without God who am I?

It is a peculiar sensation, this double-consciousness,
This sense of always looking at oneself through the eyes
Of others . . . this two-ness, an American, a Negro; two souls,
Two thoughts, two un-reconciled strivings; two warring ideals
In one dark body, whose dogged strength alone keeps it from
Being torn asunder
W.E.B. Du Bois

I Grew Up Knowing Something

Was Not Right About Being An Afrikan In America

As an elementary school pupil I wholeheartedly sang "God Bless America"
and "This is my Country" during morning assemblies. When I was a child
I thought as a child. I also remember when I stopped placing my hand over
my heart to say the Pledge of Allegiance to the flag and when I stopped
singing the Star Spangled Banner in assembly. I hadn't even reached junior
high school. I had a hole in my soul and cries that couldn't be heard. Nor
could Negro History Week console me. It just was not enough to fill the
gaping wound in my soul that I couldn't articulate at the time.

    I commend dear Mr. Carter G. Woodson for gaining a medium that
enabled society to ponder the achievements of our pigmented people. At
least we had one week out of the fifty-two to make everyone pause and
consider our contributions to the great USA built on free labor. This was
the only time during the year we could go to the front of the class to boast
of a noteworthy Black person that we admired.

Yes, I grew up knowing something was not right about living in America as an Afrikan. I felt our absence from the school history books. All the pictures in the history books were of White folks and none of them looked like me. I only remember one teacher saying that the cradle of civilization was in Mesopotamia which my parents told me was a part of Afrika

I was born in 1950, but in the sixties during the Civil Rights era I was always watching the evening news with my parents and seeing my people marching in the streets and having sit-in's to gain equal rights.

I saw the angry dogs let loose on them, the water hoses surging at them, and the night sticks hitting their heads during their peaceful demonstrations. I was just a pre-teen and it was so perplexing seeing my people kicked, beaten, bleeding, dragged and thrown in jail on my TV screen and to read of this in the newspapers.

Why were they being beaten? Was it because they wanted to be recognized as second-classed citizens in this country that their ancestors were kidnapped to come and build?

How does one reconcile these kinds of hypocrisies and still feel good about growing up in America? It was too much for my young mind to grasp. I didn't feel safe outside my home. When were they going to come after me with dogs and water hoses and nightsticks I wondered?

One sure thing the wider society didn't let us forget is that we were the descendants of those who were enslaved. Systematically they made us feel responsible for our own subjugation; only because of the color of our skin.

Growing up with this duality of race consciousness forced me to think of Afrika as my real homeland and that I didn't belong where I found myself.

In high school I often wondered how life would be if I were living in Afrika! I'd daydream about belonging to a royal family? Where do I come from in Afrika? What language should I be speaking? I began to long for the Afrikan side of me; the one that I missed by being born on the wrong side of the Atlantic Ocean. However I pondered these things in my heart more than vocalizing these feelings to anyone.

I was in high school at the time of the March on Washington. There were buses I could join to ride to D.C. but none of my friends wanted to go and my parents wouldn't allow me to travel alone not knowing anyone else going on the trip. I languished over not being able to make that trip for a long time. I should have been there.

Let me even send a shout out to Mrs. Ginsberg my Simon Gratz High School counselor who told me I wasn't college worthy. It's because of her telling me what I couldn't do that made me vow not to be another high school dropout statistic.

God's Trying To Tell You Something.

In September 1968 after high school graduation I attended James Martin Trade School and learned practical nursing. I was trained and employed at Temple University Hospital and chose to be assigned to the psychiatric unit which fascinated me.

My spiritual life was rather dormant during my teens, once out of high school and into my early twenties. My sisters were singing on the church choir and my mother was praying for me to return to the fold. They would beg me to come to church, but I lost the closeness to Spirit I experienced in childhood. I was reading horoscopes and having my palm read and responded once that God didn't talk to me when someone asked me if I believed in God? By this time I was feeling grown-up, working as an L.P.N., making my own good money and partying heartily.

I was into the night life so much that my mom said I had to move out of the house because I was becoming a bad example for my younger sisters.

I understood mother's position and I had already been saving a hope chest full of items I would need for my future apartment. I had linen, dishes, silverware, glasses, towels, furniture in lay-away etc., all in wait for when I would make a move to be on my own. I had been waiting to turn twenty-one years old in about six months to respectfully leave my parents' house and venture on my own.

While working at the hospital I met my first husband. I didn't value myself when we met; I loved him more than I loved myself. Mike was a good guy and I found it unbelievable that he would be interested in me. We had fun while the fun lasted but we were both too immature to be settling down together.

I went on a weight loss program and reduced from a size 18 to a size 12 and went with my two girlfriends Diane and Paula on a trip to Jamaica. I wanted to sit at the beautiful ocean coast and meditate on whether I should get married or not. Well I did just that and knew the answer coming to me was a resounding no but I didn't heed it. I pressured him to make plans to marry when I returned from the trip.

I didn't return to church until I decided I wanted a church wedding, not a big one but one held in the chapel with family, close friends and a big reception for about sixty people at a neighborhood social hall. Mike and I were all about boogie nights and when he danced he drew a crowd of admirers. We even moved in an apartment together before the wedding to my mother's horror.

One Sunday I accepted my mom's invitation and met her at church. I really had the wrong motive because I only wanted to meet the pastor to ask permission for our upcoming wedding to be held there.

If I were planning the day's events that would take place on this morning I first would never have worn the shortest dress I had in my closet. When the pastor came to the part of the service to ask people to come to the altar and accept Jesus as their personal savior my hand went up as if it were on a puppet string. I was sitting there pondering going up but resisting the urge. My hand was up, all eyes were on me and I felt as if I were whisked out of my seat and propelled to the front of the church faster than my feet could carry me.

I was overcome by a cloud of joy, peace, and love that I never felt before. I was asked my name and what church I was from previously but I could barely remember my own name. I was flooded with the love of God, I was so happy and it was such a beautiful experience! I walked back to my seat and sat down by my mother who was crying happy tears for her daughter who was lost but now was found.

"Take Me Back to Afrika
That is Where my People From"
Music video: Holla Blak
Power, Future & Cease Fire

What Would You Go Back To Afrika For?

This phenomenal experience rekindled my journey back to things of the spirit. I started reading the Bible passionately and attending church regularly while becoming more settled in my social life. All this was just in time before I married in August of 1973. The Bible would come to serve as my comfort on lonely nights when the newlywed stage frizzled away from our relationship about six months later.

I was now described as a person who was fanatical about the things of God. I was attending seminars of all kinds that helped me conquer personal conflicts in a Godly way. I threw away all my hot pants, miniskirts, liquor and even my record albums and made an about face on all worldly things. My party friends said what a shame it was that I was so young to have began a life of church going.

This lifestyle went on for three or four years until a young lady was admitted to the hospital psych unit exhibiting bizarre behavior saying she was being persecuted because she loved the Lord. She said all her troubles began because she loved Jesus. She lost her mind, her job, and her children were all taken away.

This shook me up because of how everyone perceived my new persona. So I remember praying to God to take his anointing off me because I didn't want to go crazy. Ever since that prayer the zealousness without knowledge has left me and that overpowering urgency I felt compelling me to eat, drink, and sleep nothing but the word of God has dissipated. Sometime I would fall asleep on my knees praying and wake up in the morning still on my knees. Now those days were over. I'm not as brow beating, and judge-mental as that time. I love my maker, my Creator! I am a worshiper of the Divine One and I pray to soar to my highest good in God and live my life as an example of the love of God.

Also at work one day I met an angel. There was a young Black male patient who was hospitalized due to too much stress from his academic studies. He told me about Temple University looking for students for their New Career Ladders program to learn social work administration

At the same time a certain doctor on our unit looked down on the contribution nurses made towards the rehabilitation of patients. He frequently stated it was only the doctors, therapists and social workers who really helped the patients get well. This motivated me to investigate the college scheme that gave academic credit for life experience.

I called for an application, applied for the program and was called in for an interview before a panel. I didn't keep the appointment because I was afraid, too shy to speak up for myself. When the counselor called to follow-up I made the excuse that I was making more money as a nurse than I'd make as a social worker and that I decided to withdraw before I even started.

This counselor was a good motivator, he told me that education was something you do for yourself and was something that no one could ever take away from you. He went on to say learning is what you do to enhance yourself. He convinced me and I was welcomed into the program even without the interview.

This was during the early Seventies, January 1974 exactly when I began taking as many Pan Afrikan Studies courses as I could; and Dr. Molefi K. Asante was heading the Department at Temple University (PASCEP).

I was studying Social Administration and Pan African Studies was my minor. My Jewish counselor told me I would get a micro view of the world, I responded, haven't I lived the macro view all my life? Is there something wrong with learning my own history? He asked me if I were a member of the Black Panther Party. I didn't answer him but I looked the part with my large afro hairdo, boots, and army fatigues and in those days I was very angry about race relations in the country.

In response to my attitude he intentionally didn't turn in my request slip to take a Statistics course on a pass/fail basis. Thank God I passed the course anyway, didn't pull my cumulative grade down and I made the deans' list a couple of semesters.

At this time I began to observe how pervasive racism was in our society. This racial prejudiced system was institutionalized and imbedded in the fabric of society. You could feel it in the air, it was as thick as if it could be cut with a knife, and nearly making you develop a split personality in order to cope with it all.

Once I was so despondent over the plight of Black people all over the world and I sought counsel from one of my Afrikan professors and I cried and asked her will we learn our lessons, wake up and unify as a people for our own best interests?

She commented I would probably be one to help facilitate the process since I was so passionate about the situation. I still cry why God why? When God when?

At this time I was a twenty-three year old newlywed, a freshman in school and my loving husband accused me of marrying him so I could quit work and become a full time student. Then an opportunity to visit Afrika presented itself and I was so excited but he was not one bit interested. The trip consisted of touring four West Afrikan countries and I was eager to travel with them.

"What would you go back to Afrika for, he asked? They didn't want us; that's why we're here in the USA. So I declined the trip to visit West Afrikan countries in 1974 only because hubby didn't want to go.

My friend Jeannette and her husband Walter (May he rest in peace.) made the trip instead and I took on a nursing position working at night while studying as a day student. When you have the luxury of being a full time student count your blessings and thank your God for the privilege. That is a life of pure freedom to have time off from the responsibilities of life just to study and educate your-self.

I studied three years straight through the summers and squeezed in some evening classes before my night duty shift. I managed to graduate in three years and walked down the aisle for my bachelors' degree in May 1977, while four months pregnant.

"My hope for my children must be
That they respond to the still small
Voice of God in their own heart"
Andrew Young

It's A Boy!

By now my hubby and I had separated because as he put it at the marriage counselor's office "he had fallen out of love with me." I earlier decided since the relationship might not work out-I secretly stopped taking the birth control pills so I could get pregnant. I wanted to have a child out of this union. I would frequently care for my sister Sylvia's daughter and when Tameka and I were out together-people would ask me if she were my daughter I'd lie and say yes. So it was time I had a child of my own. However I didn't know I was pregnant when we first parted so we tried to reunite for the sake of the baby but it was a loveless relationship and we split up.

My mother and father had no brothers' and they didn't have any sons, I had the first boy born in generations. I kept my beautiful baby boy Latif Merritt Schofield born 10th November 1977 and retained hubby's last name. My son turned two years old when we parted the last time and finally divorced. I remember as his dad was leaving and I was crying. My son wiped my eyes and said to me "don't cry mommy, we'll be alright." Often if I said I didn't feel well he'd lay his hands on me and pray a simple prayer for me to feel better.

I salute every woman who had the courage to go through childbirth more than once. My experience was so painful and labor was so long, resulting in a caesarean operation with many complications that I promised myself I would never go through it again. Most women say that once the pregnancy's over you forget the pain of it all, but I never forgot.

I felt that my son was an angel sent to me from God! He really changed my life to have such a beautiful child to love and care for-so dependent upon me. I'd sit in a rocking chair and sing and read to him before and after he was born and spoiled him so that he always wanted to be held. I was so elated to have him to cherish even though the marriage didn't last. His name means gentle pleasant one from the Aramaic language which is said that Jesus spoke.

Being a mother made me even more responsible and I felt the weight of being the one dependent upon to mold, shape, and guide this little boy to be a loving, Godly, productive, active participant in the Afrikan community and the global society.

What an awesome confidence the universe had placed in me and I was humbled to be thought worthy of the sacred trust of motherhood, I loved Latif so much!

The entire family was excited to welcome a baby boy to the family. Latif had the loving arms of many aunts on both sides of the family to hold him and laps to sit on and he never wanted for anything. My sister Renee moved in with me a few years and was a big help to us and a joy to have around. His dad visited often but my father was the male role model predominantly; and those two got along very well.

I would take him for walks in his stroller around the neighborhood, take him to the playground, I photographed him all the time and thanked God for the joy of being a parent. It was me and him against the world.

His dad and I had a friendly divorce, one of those no fault quick ones that cost one hundred dollars from the neighborhood community legal service agency. I never changed my last name because the name Schofield helped me to get through certain doors when people mispronounced it as if it were a Jewish name-*Shofeld*.

However after meeting me the mistake would become obvious and I'd just chuckle to myself. Sometimes when a person prejudges you, especially over the phone it can work in your favor; it happened often with job interviews.

By the time Latif was two years old I was almost thirty, depressed, divorced, a single parent on welfare and looking for work. I applied at various places for a position in my new career of social administration and came up empty. I was in a rut.

My sister Sylvia begged me repeatedly to attend a weekend seminar with her on decision making at my alma mater in November, 1979. Sylvia was following in my footsteps learning social work too. She was also attempting to pull me out of the house and out of the blues after my marriage breakup. I reluctantly agreed to go just to please her and to stop her badgering me. God was using her as an angel and during our lunch break my life was about to change due to a spontaneous encounter between myself and a certain man I would meet.

I turned around and responded to the gentleman behind me in line at Gino's who said to me "don't look so mean." When I looked into his beautiful brown eyes, I saw a kindred soul, and it seemed I had met a long lost friend, someone I had known for eternity. I don't think I looked mean; I was looking at the overhead menu and couldn't decide what to order. I didn't fall for his line but cupid had certainly struck me with his arrow. The man introduced himself to me as John.

"Love has never cared about my schedule.
It just barges in whenever it wants."
Miriam Makeba

Love At First Sight!

Who knew fate set up this divine appointment where John and Joann would meet at a fast food restaurant on the corner of Broad Street and Columbia Ave. (Now Martin Luther King Blvd); in North Philadelphia, and thereby begin a till death do we part journey together.

We found out we had so much in common. He was in the process of finishing his last year of a bachelors degree in social work at Antioch University, and we both were determined to one day visit Afrika. I found this out during our conversation the first day we met.

I was struck by a lightning bolt of love the first time I laid my eyes on him. At first I thought he was one of the students in the seminar but I was wrong. He was in another class down the hall but I enticed him to leave his class to join me in mine. He gave me his business card and I gave him my number and we talked frequently.

As we began getting to know each other over the phone I learned John was a savvy business man, a barber instructor, and owned a barber shop on the west side of town. He discussed and debated history and politics daily with customers in his shop and he was a student during the day. He was a conscious Afrikan man who praised God for being an Afrikan.

He said his complexion was not dark enough and he wished he were blue-black like ebony wood. John was a living history book and he enjoyed talking about Afrikas' hero's who inspired the Civil Rights Movement in America. He raved about Dr. Kwame Nkrumah, Ghana's first President and how he led the movement for independence and self governance on the continent of Afrika.

He loved Dr. Patrice Lumumba the President of the Congo, and frequently quoted him saying 'We shall show the world what the Black man can do when he is allowed to work in freedom.' He lamented over the unfortunate conspiracy surrounding his death and the terrible manner he was murdered.

Nelson Mandela was John's favorite hero and he admired the power Mandela held even while behind bars for so many years. John talked about many of Afrikas' leaders as though they were his personal friends: Jomo Kenyatta, Emperor Halle Selassie, Robert Mugabe, and he spoke of various Afrikan countries as though he traveled there.

He'd say "when you read of these people and places it's just like knowing them and visiting those places" and would often say "yes I know him, yes I've been there;" but really meaning he has read of those people and places. Spirit and the ancestors were quietly and gently tugging on our heart strings with every heartbeat saying "come home."

We had our first date at a social gathering at his university and there he dropped the bomb that he was married. My heart sank but I was glad for his truthfulness. John did say he wanted a divorce, and that neither he nor his wife was happy.

I had purposely avoided any dealings with married men for twenty-nine years. I didn't want to start now but I was already hooked. I really liked John, so I gave him a time limit of one year to get his divorce and continued to see him.

John and I listened to Black Talk Radio, attended the Adunde Festival and the Unity Day annual festival on the Parkway. We visited the African American Museum and the Afrika Day activities at Penn's Landing in the summer. Probably only people who live in Philadelphia's "City of Brotherly Love" would know of these happenings which take place annually.

After a year passed and there was no divorce I had to sit John down and tell him I couldn't continue with the relationship. I had to break it off before I was too attached and too involved; I had broken my vow to God not to date someone married and was not happy about my decision.

He had passed the test by winning my sons heart too and John would often be teaching Latif some useful information, always steering him in the right direction. If my son fell down and started crying John would sing a song to him-brush off the dirt-you're not hurt, and make him laugh.

John was irresistible. He was kind, generous and really knew how to make me feel special. It broke my heart and his also; it was a most difficult decision to make. To have to break up when you're in love but I decided if he were ever divorced he could check and see if I were still available. I really loved him and it was a heart wrenching decision to make, but things couldn't continue the way they were. I cried many, many nights for the strength to live my life without him.

"What we, the colored people want, is character.
And this nobody can give us. It is something we
Must earn for ourselves"
Frederick Douglas

Life Goes On

A former classmate and good friend Queen Esther hired me as a case worker at a community center she managed in Germantown. I agonized over placing my son in day care and was very apprehensive and couldn't wait to pick him up at the end of the first day. However when I rushed in he was fine sitting under the piano playing with a little girl and asked me why I arrived so early? It eased my mind that he adapted so well, I was the one distressed of having to break the umbilical cord. By him being comfortable there I could then concentrate on my new job.

Life goes on and I found a new guy, we dated one to two years and went our separate ways while John would call once or twice in a year to say hello but he was still married and I refused to see him. I didn't date much because John had set such a high standard and I found no one else cared for me as he did. I didn't waste time and began to live a celibate lifestyle. Also I was determined not to bring different men around my son possibly causing confusion in my son's life.

I worked five years enjoying my job visiting senior citizens, assessing their need for assistance to remain independently in their homes. Since a child I've always been comfortable around older people. They have stories and wisdom to share and I like to listen.

Sorrowfully my dad fell sick and didn't tell us right away the serious symptoms he was experiencing. By the time we made an appointment to see the doctor the waiting period was three long months away. This was March 1985 and by August he passed away at sixty-seven years of age. The chemotherapy and radiation treatment made him even sicker but didn't cure the colon cancer and my dad joined the ancestors. This left a void in all of our lives especially for Latif who was eight years old at the time. He had lost his Pop-Pop and now had to learn the meaning of death.

Dad was born in Memphis, Tennessee, I don't know any of his relatives there. I only heard the name of his aunt mentioned Mrs. Mittie Bowles. I'd like to find the only family member of his I do know whose name is Carolyn Small, his niece who lives in Flint, Michigan. I've lost contact with her.

I decided to return to nursing and accepted a job with the city government hopeful of transferring to a social work position in the near future. After a few years my plan materialized and by Gods' grace I was promoted to the department of children and youth, protecting kids from being abused.

I only lasted a year and a half in the child protective services unit due to the real life horror stories I was facing on a day to day basis. I worried about children so much I was getting an ulcer, I knew it was time to save myself. I didn't have a calling to be successful in this arena.

I would never quit one job before finding a new one and I began to pray if the Almighty didn't want me to have a certain job, not to let the employer hire me. So I thank the Lord for allowing me to be hired by another social service agency to perform health needs assessments for the elderly. This time to determine the appropriate level of aid required for a person to remain at home, in an assisted living environment or at a nursing home level.

Before I left the previous agency I joined up with a coworker who prophesied about doing a great work in the community. He had lofty ideas about starting a project that would bring jobs into the area where we lived in close proximity of each other. I prayed about it a couple of years but while at a weekend retreat I attended at Blue Mountain I heard Spirit say "you can help the gentleman named_____," so I did. He was married and had a lovely wife who was physically challenged and through our business relationship we all became very close.

My mother and I became much closer after my dad made his transition. She would become depressed often so I spent a lot of time with her doing various church activities, seminars, and retreats to the Pocono Mountains. I joined an independent gospel choir and she travelled around to the different programs with us; but it broke her heart when I left her Methodist church to attend New Covenant International, a non-denominational church.

In this congregation I led the praise and worship session of our home fellowship and we did street evangelism. When the group became too large I was chosen to be the leader of the newly formed chapter. Our church had approximately 1,500 members so we broke up into smaller neighborhood study groups. Mom later forgave me and enjoyed visiting my church also. Then in August of 1991 mom died.

It was very sudden, I remember her having a fall but she stood right up as if she wasn't injured saying only her pride was hurt. The next week she was feverish, lost her appetite, and was not her normal self. She was also diabetic and I took her to see her doctor and then brought her home with me.

The next morning I took her blood pressure, it was extremely low and her pulse was so faint, I called for the rescue ambulance to come to take her to the emergency room. We were not there thirty minutes before I heard her stop answering the doctors questions when her heart apparently stopped.

There were heroic attempts to save her but she left us at just sixty-five years old. The doctor said to me "there was nothing more they could do." The death certificate said it was an accidental death because she had a broken femur from the earlier fall and a blood clot formed which became fatal. So within one week's time mom had a fall and was gone.

My mother was from Orlando, Florida, her maiden name was Gunn. A friend asked if mom's side of the family may have been resistors during slavery times, but I have no information regarding this.

My mother's oldest living relative is Mrs. Sis Ross, ninety-four years old in Orlando, Florida. She is a living miracle who stopped smoking and driving at age ninety and she still cares for herself. I have a host of cousins in Florida, Wash. D.C. and Virginia.

I was glad to have the business project to keep me occupied after losing my mom. It was one of the hardest situations I ever had to overcome although I realized she was now with the Lord; it took all my trust and faith to get through this trial.

Over the years my business buddy and I came together in the evenings and weekends doing research, writing proposals and doing the ground work to initially start a landscaping business in the warm climate and a snow removal service in the winter months.

However when the first business plan wasn't feasible he was inspired to start a courier service similar to Fed Ex and UPS. I agreed to assist and offered moral support, administrative assistance, along with a sizeable financial investment to form a corporation. All this is at the time I had my first hip replacement surgeries in February of 1992.

I recovered well and was back to work but I was finding myself alternating between two careers that were both the kind that burn you out quickly, nursing and social work but it was the volumes of paperwork that made the jobs monotonous.

I was caught up in the rat race of survival-on the merry-go-round of going to work and coming home week after week, feeling uninspired on the job. Millions of people are caught up like this, but can you call this living? It's really a slow death march. I used to jokingly say to co-workers that somewhere, someone was living my dream life, reading at the beach, watching the sunset while feeling the cool ocean breeze. Still Afrika was softly bidding me to come home.

"I'm walking" yes indeed, and I'm talking' about you and me,
"I'm hoping that you'll come back to me."
Antoine "Fats" Domino

Back In Love Again!

My life was a bit exciting due to the part time project that was materializing and would soon give sub-contract courier jobs to qualified folks in the community just like we planned. With the Most High on our side a contract would be forthcoming to deliver parcels to banks in the area.

I hadn't talked to John in a couple of years and had not seen him for over ten years but never stopped thinking of him. One day to my surprise he called and asked if I were involved in a relationship and I was not. He then asked could he see me to tell me the good news, he's "free" after an amicable divorce. This was good news to my ears! I shouted and praised the Lord. Thank you, thank you Lord.

John's timing was perfect! I needed his help and net-working skills with the community project, and on a personal level I was sure we were still compatible as if there had been no separation after so many years. I was glad for his friendship again and experienced letting someone go who comes back to you when you're meant for each other. I was ecstatic! God is so good!

John joined our inner city development project and was an asset to the courier company that became the first Afrikan owned in the Tri-State area, (Philadelphia, New Jersey, and Delaware). He knew dynamic people and brought them to join us which helped us accomplish our goals. We began our first and only contract with the Federal Reserve Bank in Philadelphia on the same day of the Million Man March in Wash. D.C. The couriers went to work while John represented them at the march. He didn't wear comfortable shoes and returned home using someone's cane due to fallen arches; but he was thrilled to be included in that historic event.

Although our courier company was licensed to operate in all 50 States and had a ninety-nine percent near perfect on time-no loss record for deliveries, the project was a short lived success. The contract only lasted a year. It was the same old story of locking out a minority owned business even when our prices were cheaper and we worked harder for less. Senator Foglietta however managed to herald an honorable Congressional Record citation for our efforts in developing jobs for our neighborhood citizens. We were all proud of the recognition as if it were a pat on the back by God!

Reluctantly, I had to fire John as a directive from my business partner because he took on a part-time job with one of our delivery sites, and my business partner felt it was a conflict of interests. So John went to work for the other company full-time and even retired with them some years later. I soon after relinquished my shares and withdrew from the community project for medical reasons.

My son Latif and John continued to get along well. On Saturdays they'd go out to breakfast and have man to man time alone. John was his barber and he also taught those skills to my son. John was a surrogate dad who considered it his moral obligation to help steer Latif in the right direction in life.

Suddenly, my dearest sister Sylvia passed away in November 1998 of a diabetic coma. It was such a shock! We had become very close and enjoyed each other's company, shopping and socializing together. She was planning to marry her first husband for the second time but she vanished and was gone too soon.

Immediately after Sylvia passed, a dear friend Kelly died of Multiple Sclerosis. Both of them were nearly forty years old and too young to die, I thought. I was very hurt by their passing and it made me want to begin living my life more fully moment by moment. There were things I wanted to do in life and I began to feel life was so short.

John and I still longed for the motherland. We weren't "in the culture" as they say, but Afrika was calling us. We still wanted to see Afrika, hear Afrika, touch Afrika, feel Afrika, and taste AFRIKA!

I was blessed to take part in the Million Women's March held in our city and I went alone when some friends declined to attend at the last minute. I was physically challenged and not walking well, dragging my right leg but I was there and carried a folding chair to sit on as I joined in with other like-minded women from all across the country on the Philadelphia Parkway. I was glad to be counted in the number of attendees of an historic occasion that rainy day Oct. 25, 1997.

John said his desire to visit Afrika went all the way back to when he was a young boy selling newspapers on the corners of South Philadelphia. He said there were many Afrikan-owned newspapers in his day and he read them all, he was born in 1931.

He remembered reading of Marcus Garvey and the Black Star Shipping Line, when Black folks (colored then) were talking about going back to Afrika. Jim Crow practices were rampant during his formative years growing up and John said he always felt a sense of not belonging in America because of the racial prejudice. He described feeling alienated, separated and constrained; at the same time he learned to succeed against the odds and made the best of his lot as a Black man in America.

When he was young he said he would do any legal work to keep jingles in his pocket. As a young boy he sold shopping bags and newspapers. He worked as a delivery boy, and he shined shoes. He pushed his age up to enlist into the army when he was only 15 years old. He said the military was the best thing that ever happened to him because he gained the discipline he needed for life. Even though the army was segregated then-he withstood the indignities he suffered. John travelled to Germany and had the title 'Attaché' with a constabulary branch of the army police. This was a great position of responsibility he held at such a young age.

Once he returned home from the military, Campbell's Soup Company employed him. He worked for the U.S. Steel Co., Curtis Publishing House, and the U.S. Postal Service. John said he worked with the railroad, a moving company, as a meat handler, construction worker, and he made lawn furniture at an aluminum factory.

He had been a doorman and security guard. In a certain hospital he started as a cook and was promoted to a managerial position in their central supply department. All this he said he experienced before he enrolled into barber school and college, before I ever knew him. This is how my John became knowledgeable about so many things. He needed a larger place to spread his wings and let out all the talents that were locked up inside him waiting to burst forth. America never offered him the opportunity to be all he could be.

Although he had a good life and plenty of experience from a host of jobs, he never broke through that "glass ceiling" that forces one to remain in a certain income class. John and I were of the working poor class trying to get to the middle class. We were not above working two or three jobs if needed. John had a wealth of knowledge from the various jobs he held throughout his sixty-seven years of living in the USA.

He was a courier in the day time, a barber in the evening, and a doorman at a ritzy apartment building at night. He was a man of many talents that needed expression.

Yes when I met John his head and his heart was in Afrika. He was a proud Afrikan man. He said he always knew he would set his feet on Mother Afrikas' soil someday. John and I had discussions all the time and debated about what is it in those of us who feel we have to get to Afrika? Why is this longing so strong in some and not in others? I don't know, now I'm asking you?

Is Afrika's imprint planted stronger in some Diaspora's DNA than in others?

When I speak of Diaspora, I'm referring to the descendants of those who left the continent of Afrika involuntarily via the Trans Atlantic Slave Trade and their descendants.

Why do people who profess to be "in the culture" never make it over to the continent? Is Afrika more than geography and maybe a state of mind? Is it possible for there to be only one person in a family can feel the connection to the motherland so strongly, while the rest of the family members think that one person strange?

Why do some Afrikan Americans act insulted when the subject of visiting Afrika is brought up? You remember Brother Malcolm X said "we left our minds in Afrika." Sometimes it's a very touchy subject. I wonder why?

We do have to reconcile some painful realities when accepting our "Afrikan-ness" and identify with the mother continent. We had to face many realities of our Afrikan heritage 'the good, the bad, and the ugly.' It is not my intention to give a history lesson here, but we faced the ugly fact that our own people had a hand in assisting the slave dealers in buying slaves.

"The European slave dealers did not generally go into the interior of Africa to buy slaves. They had agents who brought the slaves mainly from the chiefs and brought them down to the European castles on the coast. Several African Kingdoms went to war against each other simply to win more slaves to sell to the Europeans." Yes, this was the most terrible truth for us to come to terms with.[1]

Man's inhumanity to his fellow man is vile. The love of money is the root of all evil. These deeds were certainly crimes against humanity. I went through my time of bitterness against all those involved in the travesty of the "Trans Atlantic Slave Holocaust." I won't generalize that all Europeans are evil nor are all Afrikans evil.

Evil has no color and is perpetrated by persons who refuse to live at the Higher Vibration of Christ Consciousness that is available to everyone from the One Source of Love and Light, Our Creator. Suffice it to say I had to let bitterness go because it was too heavy of a burden for me to carry.

There is a Supreme Being who reigns over all the affairs of the universe and is able to execute righteous justice. Everyone receives a return on the fruits of their deeds.

I rest my case and forever honor the memory of my ancestors. The more I release resentment, the more I am free to love in the present moment.

Moreover we all have to resolve to "never, never, never let slavery happen again in any form' as Nelson Mandela has stated.

The beautiful part of my Afrikan heritage is I know we have a glorious past; royal roots and an ancient civilization that many conspire to bury, lie about and try to keep secret. Many different cultures sat at the feet of our Afrikan Kings and Queens in Kemet, Ancient Ghana, Mali and Songhai. They marveled at our sciences, architecture, agriculture, mathematics, and philosophy and we taught them all.

We have the greatest stories never told and our own historians: John Henry Clarke, Dr. Asa Hilliard (both of blessed memory), Dr. Leonard Jeffries and Dr. James Smalls, Anthony T. Browder to name a few, are pulling the covers off the falsehoods that are being perpetrated against our

---

[1]   West Africa and Europe, A New History For Schools and Colleges Book 2 F.K. Buah, pages 58-59

magnificent history by letting our glorious truths be known. These are some of our Afrikan heroes!

Yes John and I talked about the state of Afrikan affairs on and on into the wee hours of the night sometimes. The passion I felt for going home was so strong I could feel Afrikas' soil, so deep that it seemed to pulsate in my cells. I could hear the drumbeat, and smell the ocean and taste the mango. I would feel this longing come and go throughout my life, it would ebb and flow.

The years after leaving college, working in civil service, the corporate world, after marriage and divorce, facing the challenges of single parenting, I myself lost sight of the personal hopes and dreams I once set for myself. Thank God this one rose from the ashes. Praises to Our Creator! Who divinely brought John back to me and thankfully he possessed the same wish to go home to Mother Afrika, which rekindled my desires.

"Can't Nothing make your life work
If you ain't the architect"
Terry McMillian

Take Me To Afrika And Let's Get Married!

Take me to Afrika and let's get married! Who put those words into my mouth? I hadn't pre-planned to say this, yet there it was out of my mouth! It seemed as if someone else had spoken through the deepest part of me, as John answered "I sure will." Yes I would love a new life in Afrika, love to be married there, longed to get in touch with the Afrikan side of myself and now that the thought was spoken out in the open it felt good to have said it. That was the beginning of our focusing our sights on making our way home to Afrika.

The occurrences of close family and friends dying made me want to live life and do the things that I really longed to do without delay. I think I spoke that request to John from my unconscious self and now we were going to pray and take the first step of faith into the unknown.

I maintained that for those of us in the Diaspora who desire to return to Mother Afrika should be able to choose any place on the continent to settle and call it home. We are betwixt and between two worlds. Our ancestors were kidnapped and carried off to America. We are Afrikans' born in America as my sister Nia said to me one day and it seemed to snap me out of a hypnotic and co-opted state of mind.

I know that there is DNA testing going on now that can probably tell us where our roots are likely to be from. However we felt the entire continent belonged to us to decide wherever we wanted to go.

John said just throw a dart at the map of Afrika and let's go. However we did do our research and sought Spirit for guidance and narrowed our choice down to Ghana. We considered Nigeria and South Afrika but we choose Ghana because it was a peaceful country and English is the national language. John said rather that Ghana chose us.

We went to the library and read books on Ghana formally called the Gold Coast. We logged onto the internet to see what we could find and there was a good amount of information to research. We visited a Ghanaian Association of the Delaware Valley meeting, and talked to anyone we heard had visited Ghana. We bought travel books on Ghana and ferreted out as much as we could to have an idea of what to expect upon our arrival in Ghana. We started keeping a scrap book of articles about Ghana.

We met a lady outside a supermarket asking for donations to take her students to Ghana. She was Ann Guise a teacher who was the head of the "Bright Lights"; an inner city public school program and she said Kwame Toure named the group. She traveled with many junior high school students over the years reuniting them with their Afrikan roots.

We went to one of their after school-activities; and found these young people to be some of the smartest and gifted students we'd come across in a long time. They orated and sang so well. The surprising thing was my nephew Ranell and his sister Martia were participating on this day. I know that made my ancestors happy, and I was sure a proud auntie.

At the same time while at this community gathering John met an old friend named Bamba Ra who said he traveled extensively in West Afrika. He had a lot to say. When I told him that I wanted a home in front of the ocean, he said "there's plenty of it waiting there for you." I took that as a sign from God. Bamba Ra and his wife Raya were fashion designers and would later design the outfits we would wear for our going away party. This would be our farewell-to-America party.

We learned of an exhibit at the University of Pennsylvania on Canaan and Ancient Israel but it was the last day and we couldn't get to see it and we were very disappointed. Egypt is part of Afrika but the media and others are trying to persuade us all that there's a place called the Middle East. What ever happen to North Afrika! When I read the Bible I believe that it's a story about Afrikans and Afrika; I make it personal to me by reading it through an Afrikan lens but I leave the debate to our historians.

The excitement was mounting! John and I couldn't think of anything else. We ate, slept and dreamt of Afrika. When we told people we were moving to Afrika the responses we received were "you must be crazy!" Most folks didn't believe us, or asked "why would you want to do that?" The few who could identify with us and the motherland encouraged us to go for it!

John already possessed his passport so I went to process mine. On the application where they ask the destination I wrote Ghana, the home of my ancestors. We read that there were seventy-two slave castles and forts in Ghana.

We had the feeling that if our roots were not from Ghana our ancestors could have most certainly passed through Ghana's Door of No Return. Where the application asked for the duration of stay I wrote "Until death." With half my life already spent in America I was exhilarated to live the last half of my life in Afrika.

I soon had my passport in my hands!

"Go within every day and find the inner strength
So that the world will not blow your candle out"
Katherine Dunham

10

Did We Miss God?

Sometimes faith is tested. You have your dreams and all seems to be going well and then wham! You're broadsided, literally! You wonder what's going on! Did we miss God? John was involved in a head on collision auto accident. The driver of another car hit him while he was on his way to pick me up and drive me to a doctor appointment.

Someone in the crowd was able to get him to unlock the car door, and give a phone number of someone to call and the person called me. I was stunned, but I didn't forget to pray. I asked my neighbor Mr. Valentine to drive me to the emergency room to see him. When we reached there he was on a stretcher, in a neck brace and receiving IV fluids. He could talk but he was in pain while the doctor ordered a CAT scan and other tests to see the extent of his injuries.

Doubts entered my mind and a negative voice was talking in one ear saying "you aren't going anywhere, now look at him; he's going to be paralyzed." Ah "But God!" God was talking in my other ear and in my heart saying, "All will be well, don't fear, have faith!" With those comforting words I left John in good hands, while I rushed to the subway train to the other side of town to keep my medical appointment.

I was scheduled for hip-replacement surgery the following week. I opted to deposit my own blood for my surgery and this was my last pint to give. Somehow I calmly got through all this and returned to the hospital to see John. By then he had all the scans, X-rays, and lab work that was ordered; and we were waiting the results. We wouldn't know anything until the next day because visiting hours were over and I had to leave. I wanted to spend the night right there beside him but wasn't allowed. I reassured him to rest well, pray, and believe that the Lord would bring him out of this situation in good health.

The next day I arrived at the hospital to meet the doctor with John and hear the verdict. He said there would have to be surgery on his neck from vertebrae four through seven, take them out and put in metal braces and pins. I felt like I was punched in the stomach. Oh no, Father I don't want them cutting on his spine I shouted within myself.

The doctor showed us the x-rays and we could even see with our naked eyes where the problem was. He assured us he had performed hundreds of this procedure and his recovery would be good. John had the final say and his operation was scheduled for the same day and the same time that mine was scheduled for in a different hospital across town the next week.

We liked doing things together but having operations on the same day and time: this was too much togetherness for me! However we cast out all fear and put our trust in our Maker to bring us to an expected end. We believed we would both come through our surgeries well and live to give God the glory. We had a vision and a mission that we knew was unstoppable; it may have looked otherwise. Our going home was birthed in the spirit realm and we couldn't let go of that dream no matter what. We kept our hands in God's hand.

My friend Jeannette (An angel in my life since I was a teenager.) informed me of a friend of hers named Ted who was planning a group trip to Ghana. She said he traveled there several times a year donating to various schools. We called Ted and there was a meeting scheduled for the next day 18th February to discuss the trip.

John told me not to visit him in the hospital but to attend the meeting in Southwest Philadelphia. He wanted me to go and find out everything about their plans for the trip to Ghana. I went to the meeting at Kiesha's apartment where there were a dozen people gathered and I learned they planned to arrive in Ghana July 4th, 1999. This was spiritually symbolic for us to leave on Independence Day!

This time we would be getting our independence for real, going out to a place that God would show us, going home to the continent our ancestors were stolen away from, going back to get our culture, our language, our roots, and our destiny!

There were Panafest and Emancipation Day Programs scheduled which are cultural, historical and geared towards the advancement of Pan Afrikan ideals. It all sounded so interesting and added more fuel to the fire to travel with the group. A visit to South Afrika for a week was even on their itinerary. Wow maybe we'll see Nelson Mandela! I was wishfully thinking.

Ted visited John while he was in the hospital to encourage him to keep the faith to make the trip. This was February 1999 and we were five months away from the July 3rd date to leave the country. We truly wanted to go with Ted's group because of the timing, but our savings were not enough to purchase the tickets. They had a monthly payment plan to have the tickets paid by the end of May 1999, with a total cost of $2,900.00 for both our tickets. John and I hadn't paid anything as yet.

It was time for me to check into University of Pennsylvania Hospital and John was in Temple Hospital with both our surgeries scheduled for the next day. This was the second time I had to have both hips replaced due to arthritis. They don't usually repair both hips at once.

I had the right hip fixed earlier in December of 1998 and now the left hip had to be repaired. It wasn't easy but I was told I'd be bedridden if I didn't have the surgery because my pelvis bone would collapse. The prayer of faith was not working for my situation, so I had to use the God given medical professional expertise available for my healing.

What a mighty God we serve! The Lord our healer! The two of us had to lie flat a couple of days, and we both were anxious not being able to see each other but we talked frequently over the phone. John did well as the days went by that he was actually kicked out of the hospital. He was found in the stairwell smoking and discharged from the hospital.

I assume they felt if he could get out of bed to go and smoke he could as well be at home recovering. John was sent home to finish recuperating with a home health nurse to visit him once weekly.

One of the hospital staff gave John the business card of a lawyer friend another angel who took the case, saying it was a no contest situation. The person driving the car that hit him was at fault and both parties were well insured. All John had to do was wait it out. You know these kinds of cases could go on for years before any settlement is decided.

I was still an inpatient when my doctor dropped a bombshell that I should stay in for an additional six weeks of rehab-training and a series of intravenous antibiotics. You have got to be kidding me was my response. He was very serious as he explained running a catheter up through my left arm to my heart. This site would be used to give me antibiotics on a long term basis. He wanted to be sure there was no trace of infection in my body whatsoever.

When I told him I had plans to travel to Afrika to live, he then thought I was joking! Do you think that it's wise after a surgery of this nature he asked? I told him I was already there in spirit and it was just my physical body talking to him. Yes I assure you, I will go to Ghana and I'll send X-rays every year to keep in touch. I agreed to the antibiotic treatment and physical rehab and was transferred to a hospital closer to home.

Johns' first week home alone from the hospital didn't go well at all. He wasn't taking his medicine properly and started over medicating, not eating well and having falls. I had to ask my neighbors Leon and Earnestine (Angels) to check on him and prepare meals for him. The visiting nurse organized his meds for him and the next week he improved.

This time was very difficult for me to not be there when he needed me to care for him. As soon as John was feeling better, everyone knew because he would prepare lunch for me, take public transportation, and bring it to the hospital when he was supposed to be at home resting. He was still wearing his neck brace and he would come and sit all day with me. He was so kind, loved feeding me and no one could make him rest when he had his mind set on doing something.

All these weeks in the hospital I placed a picture of a beautiful house sitting in front of an ocean on the wall and I meditated on it believing that it would manifest for us in Afrika. On one certain day while I was wheeled from rehab to my room; a certain gentleman got on the elevator. A voice within says to me "ask him, has he ever been to Ghana?" I questioned in my head thinking that I didn't know this man he'll think I'm crazy. The voice says "ask him now, before he gets off the elevator and you'll never see him again!"

I obeyed and asked, Sir have you ever visited Ghana? He replied no I haven't but my wife has. She and a Ghanaian lady worked together as nurses and the lady has returned to Ghana and built a guesthouse. I'll call my wife and ask her to fax me the information and bring it to your room. Great! I gave him my room number.

When John visited I told him all about this special happening and we waited for him. Just as John said "he won't come" and was about to leave; the brother came bopping in the room and introduced himself as Lee J. Harold and he had the brochure in his hand. He went on to tell us his wife and daughter visited Mrs. Anastasia Hooper at Fairhill Guesthouse in Cape Coast, Ghana. There were even some video tapes of their trips we could view. We were elated with the possibility of seeing Ghana on these tapes and we said as soon as I was discharged we'd get in touch with him.

Physical therapy took lots of patience and determination but having the goal to travel made it so much easier for me to persevere through it. I was discharged with less than three months to go before our deadline. I was using a cane to walk and John completed his course of therapy and could drive again, glory to God. His car was a total wreck after the accident so he rented a car. We began to make clear plans for our journey to the motherland.

I think that the human race does command its own destiny
And that destiny can eventually embrace the stars.

Lorraine Hansberry

11

A Blessing In Disguise

We started making definite plans to leave. We entertained Ted, his mother, and others in the group at our house a couple of times so we could get more information on life in Ghana. We called Ann at Fairhill Guesthouse and spoke to her husband Ricky who told us she was visiting (of all places) America and in New Jersey. He gave us her number, we contacted her but we never met because she was too busy.

We wrote to her when she returned to Ghana and poured out our hearts about our coming to Ghana to stay. We asked if we could have our mail sent to her P.O. Box number temporarily and she agreed. We sent for housing information in Ghana from the State Housing Development Corp., Regimanuel Gray Ltd. and received information packets from them both. We called an international relocation service of realtors who find real estate in various countries, but they had no listings in Afrika.

We looked into international medicine clinics for the vaccines we had to get and the costs, we found they must be administered one month in advance. The yellow fever vaccine which was the only mandatory one cost $50.00 and you must keep the yellow card as proof. However Hepatitis A and B shots were recommended at $60.00 each along with Typhoid shot for $45.00 and last but not the least the tetanus shot for $20.00.

At the same time the office visit was $40.00 in which they would give us malaria tablets to take two weeks prior to traveling. Most people just get the mandatory yellow fever vaccination and the malaria pills. We decided to get all but the hepatitis B vaccine because we didn't intend to have intimate relations with anyone else. We would wind up paying $215.00 each for this medical protection, but felt prevention was better than cure.

We had a lot of questions too. What about dual citizenship? We heard there's free land for Afrikan Americans, is this true? Can we get married there? What necessities to pack? Can we bring a laptop and use the 110 amp? Are there supermarkets there like we are used to? Is there a Western Union there? Where to get travel visa applications? How much does it cost to rent a house in Accra? What about banking and wire transfers? Some questions were answered and yet some we would have to wait and see.

Time was moving fast, our friends were convinced by our actions that we were dead serious and some began to have people they knew visited Afrika call us and some shared their videos with us. All this was very helpful even though some of the videos were about the Gambia and South Afrika. Any information about Afrika was gratefully received and we happily enjoyed them all.

We started visiting Afrikan Art shops and talking with owners. One day we visited the Merchant of Alkebulan and spoke to the owner Josh. During the conversation it came out that he knew Johns' son Jason and how to locate him.

John hadn't seen Jason in years because he lived with the mother from a previous relationship. We looked him up and what a beautiful reunion it was for the two of them. Jason was now the owner of a barber shop and barber just like his dad. We visited his place of business and he gave us his best wishes for our new life in Ghana. John had two other adult sons and a daughter from his first marriage whom he said would not be happy about him leaving the country. Their names are John Jr., Cecilia, and David.

Jeannette introduced us to another friend of hers named Ama who was married to a Ghanaian. We went to meet her and waited for her husband Kwame (Charles Owusu Fordjour) to come home from work. She said that he would never believe this story of a couple wanting to leave America to go to Ghana for the first time and don't know anyone in the country; yet saying they're going home.

When Kwame arrived, we told him our plans, he believed we were serious and opened up to us. He told us all about Ghana's chop bars, open gutters, how buses don't leave the station until they're full, water is rationed, frequent electricity shut-offs and other things that would have discouraged anyone else.

He invited us over again for dinner and he would cook a Ghanaian meal for us. This dish we would come to know and love called red-red with fish, plantain and beans in tomato sauce. Thank God we didn't also have our taste buds stolen from us. We ate it all and asked for second rounds.

Kwame gave us the best advice ever, re: our trip to Ghana; Accept what you see, don't judge, don't compare: Just accept! He said Ghana is the way it is until Ghanaians themselves want to change it." This advice is true to social work teachings: one must accept the cultural differences of people and not judge them to be right or wrong. This is one of the fundamentals of getting along with people all around the world. Everyone has their own uniqueness. Give respect and respect will be given in return. We believed we'd be able to adapt!

We called on Lee J Harold to get hold of the videos he had of Ghana but he kept delaying us wanting to watch them with us but not having the time to do so. We were persistent in calling and leaving messages at his house until he relented to give us the tapes to take to our home to watch. I guess he was afraid we wouldn't return them to him. After all he didn't really know us. We went to his home and met his lovely wife Netfa and daughter Nia. We didn't know at the time that this was the beginning of a long lasting friendship between us. Their videos were great for seeing everyday life in Ghana. Ann was on the tapes showing the land where Fairhill Guesthouse was built, so we saw the beginning stages of the place we would later call heaven. We made a copy of the tapes and returned them of course.

Now mind you, we were making all these plans and haven't paid any money down for our tickets and the deadline was approaching. We still didn't have the lump sum of money. Yet we see ourselves packed and on the plane and in Ghana. It seemed to us as long as we kept busy plugging away towards our mission, believing . . . it would happen. We believed God wanted to give us the desire of our hearts so we started packing! Ann told us to buy the square dish boxes from U-haul because they fit better on the aircraft. As if we didn't have enough to do I had the big idea to have a going away party.

We scheduled the party for the 12th of June, 1999 and my sister Nia printed the invitations. We asked guests to dress in traditional Afrikan garb and bring something we could take with us to give to schools or hospitals. We had it catered by Sherreal, and called on some Afrikan drummers and dancers. We invited poets, and had a story teller for the children. Muriel Feelings from the Pan Afrikan Studies Department at Temple University graced us with her presence and gave some of her own authored books.

The food was good and we all drank champagne. So many friends, co-workers, and family all brought gifts so much so that we filled up six of those dish boxes full of donations. One look in the backyard you would think that you were already in Afrika by the sights and the sounds. It was a great going away party! One of which we had many fond memories. So many guests; so much love poured out. Thank you father for such a beautiful day!

Leave it to me to add something else to the plate. I wanted to take my nieces and nephews away to Atlantic City for a weekend vacation for sort of a forget-me-not party. I wanted to talk to them about staying close as a family. I asked them to promise to get together at least once a year even if it was just a cookout at one of their houses. I tried to explain how I felt Afrika calling me home and why I had to answer the call. I hoped some of them may want to visit one day.

John was agreeable for me to do whatever I wanted to do. I always had him taking me somewhere I could see an ocean, a river or a lake. So now he and I, William Thomas, William Randolph, Isaiah, Ranell, Avery, LaShanna, Dominique, Delia, Karimu, Martia, little Jasmine who could hardly talk yet; and Gail a neighbor to help chaperone, were off to the sea shore.

We rented a van with a driver for Gail and the children and John and I drove behind them and started toward our adventure. We were all excited and had a wonderful time on the 22nd floor of The Flagship Resort facing the ocean and enjoying the pool and Jacuzzi. We rode bicycles on the boardwalk and played in the arcades.

I enjoyed them so much and was so glad to have the opportunity to spend time with them before we left for Afrika. Their ages were between three and twelve years at the time; I was too pleased when my friend Louise a retired teacher decided to join us to help keep the group of children in check.

When it was time to return home I had to send the children on home with Gail because John became ill. We would years later find out that John would become hypoglycemic from not eating well. John enjoyed his beer and smoked cigarettes of which I hounded him constantly to stop. Of course the nagging only made the situation worse.

This was something I really had to come to grips with before taking this trip to travel half way around the world with him. All of a sudden John could pass out from low blood sugar and have to be rushed to the hospital for IV fluids. Once he received the fluids he was revived and able to drive us home.

This was the second time before we left for Ghana that this happened. I had to ask myself did I love him enough to go through this "in sickness and in health till death do you part?" Obviously the answer was yes because here I am writing this book about our life and times in Ghana. Thank God that I had a Practical Nursing background which would come in handy about two dozen times over the nine and half years we spent together in Afrika.

We hadn't heard any word from the lawyer and we spent our money doing all the preliminary things that had to be done for our trip. We sent our passports with Ted to give to someone who traveled to Washington D.C. to obtain visas from the Ghanaian Embassy. We didn't feel secure turning our passports over but we had to trust all would be well and applied for the multi-entry visa which cost $50.00 each which lasts for five years.

When the person returned from Wash. D.C., mission accomplished with visas granted, Ted wanted to hold all the passports himself. He wanted to hand them in all together as we traveled. We didn't like that idea but acquiesced to him as the group leader.

Kofi and I wanted to keep our passports and air tickets in our possession and take an airport limo to New York to spend the night at an airport hotel. We wanted to be at the airport ready to go. However Ted talked us out of that too saying he was sending a van to pick us up the same morning of the flight. We didn't have to worry about anything except the time to pay for the air tickets was overdue.

I don't think the Lord tired of me thanking Him for the ticket money to come on time. We were "Believing those things that are not as though they were;" as the Bible says. We saw ourselves on the plane and touching down in Ghana safely. I was rather concerned how John would fare on the flight because this was his first air flight at the age of 67. He never wanted to fly before and even when he was in the military he opted to travel overseas by ship. This was one trip he really desired and assured me he would be okay. He wanted to be at the airport early with bells on and so did I.

"All things work together for good to those who love God, to those who are called according to His purpose, Romans 8:28 NKJV. That one phone call we've been waiting for came. "Mr. Childs come into our office and sign off on your settlement check." I thought I heard angels in the background singing the "Halleluiah Chorus." We were sure singing Oh Happy Day!

We knew it was not possible to reconnect to the Motherland as if we were born there; but as much as possible we wanted to reclaim as much of the culture as we could that had been stolen from us. It was not our intention to be tourists.

We wanted to give to Ghana, not take or rape Ghana's resources. Our research taught us of the rich minerals and natural resources found in Ghana like gold, diamonds, cocoa, manganese, bauxite, and timber. These types of investments were out of our league. We hadn't decided how to add value to Ghana but we knew we wanted to be a help to the people in our immediate locale and its economy.

John and I would attempt to build bridges between ourselves and our new found brothers and sisters and form a cultural exchange. We would have to wait until our arrival and survey the landscape to see exactly what options we'd have. We even had our first email address as johnjoannGodsquad@aol.com. All we wanted to do was to go around doing good deeds wherever we went and help some people to take care of their families by creating small income opportunities.

We just wanted to do God's will and for Him to bless us so we could be a blessing to others. This was truly our hearts desire. It seemed we arrived at the lawyer's office without our feet touching the ground and the date was June 23rd, 1999. The secretary said that she worked at this same law office for 12 years and had never seen a case settled as fast as his was. After sharing with the lawyer his percentage, John signed for a good lump sum of money!

God you are wonderful, my Lord you are excellent! Our answer was on the way even before we called on the Lord! The two of us never discussed how much we thought the case would be worth. We never called the lawyer to ask anything, we just waited on the Lord. We knew we needed enough money for the air tickets and some spending money to settle down with. However this blessing was over and above what we could ever ask or think!

We were so full of gratitude to the Creator for sparing Johns' life and that he came through the surgery and rehabilitation successfully; there was no amount of money worth his good health. This money would certainly be enough for us to manage our new life and set down some roots in Mother Ghana.

Now it appeared that the car accident turned out to be a blessing in disguise, because we'd surely still be trying to save the money for our airfare. We don't understand why the cost to travel to Afrika is so high? There are places that are farther away and cost less to travel to by air. Certainly it appears to be just another stumbling block and hurdle for the Afrikan to jump and deter people from making the trip.

At last we could call Ted to come for the ticket money. The travel agent had been frustrated with him because of our delay, now everybody would be happy. We were already packed, we had our vaccines; and our visas, although Ted was still holding onto the passports and discouraged us from spending the night at an airport hotel in New York because he had transportation arranged. By God's Grace we would be ready to fly in eleven days. We had small details to tend to, some debts to pay off, some last minute shopping and last goodbyes to say to some folks.

The rest of the days sped by as we did our best to dot all i's and cross all t's to be sure that we completed everything on our "to do" list. The night before we left I could hardly sleep. I was flooded with emotions of excitement for the adventure ahead and sadness for the parting from family and friends. Afrika was pulling me closer and there was no turning back now. We're going forward in faith that God would lead us to the place where we're supposed to be, which would further be revealed as we took our first step. John has had a made up mind from the beginning and felt akin to Abraham going out to a new place that God would show him.

Kiesha phoned to say be ready at 8am tomorrow morning for the van to pick us up to go to the airport.

"Just as a tree without roots is dead,
A people without history or cultural
Roots also becomes' a dead people."
Malcom X

12

Bye-Bye, America

Saturday July 3, 1999 was the day of our departure. 7a.m. our neighbors were out to see us off and friends Queen and Ruth were with us as we waited to be picked up and taken to New York JFK Airport. Our next door neighbors Valentine and Earnestine (now of Blessed Memory) took pictures and joked with us about how we were going to eat monkey meat with our hands and live on trees. They said things in jest that many people believed about Afrika.

My son Latif was twenty-one years of age, working for Blue Cross Medical Insurance Company and he was making good money and was able to care for himself. I felt at this time he could be left on his own. At least he behaved as if he were grown and didn't need me anymore. He hadn't spent enough time with me to get the details of how to manage things in our absence. He seemed not to believe we were really going unless he saw us off to the airport. He didn't express any negativity about my move but seemed rather indifferent. We would both experience a deep loss from not being able to see each other on a day to day basis-it's been only the two of us for most of his life..

I actually thought he'd be happy we were going because he'd have the house to himself and wouldn't have me to hound him anymore. Now I was leaving the house and all it entailed to Latif. I deemed him ready for the responsibility.

We purchased a computer and internet service and a fax machine for the house so we could communicate easier between continents. John didn't like it that I wanted to pay the mortgage for a year when we left. It was only $338.00 a month and our son was working, but I guess I had guilt issues about leaving and I over-compensated in this way.

My deceased mother was the person who kept the family coming together for holidays and special occasions and I tried to follow in her shoes doing the same thing as the oldest child. Since I was leaving it was thought the mantle should pass to my sister Renee but she said she didn't want it. I hoped she was joking. I love my precious sisters Renee, Nia, my niece Tameka whom I love like a daughter and all of my nieces and nephews and I was going to miss them all so much.

I prayed they would understand that my destiny was calling me. I was not abandoning them but actually going to prepare a place for them and who ever wanted to explore their horizons outside the borders of the USA was invited to the legacy that would surely manifest. I didn't understand it all myself. I only knew the ancestors were calling me and I had to go to Afrika.

We were still waiting 8am, 9am, 10am,11am, when Alan the driver arrived very irritable and Donna and Rita who were also going on the trip screamed at us "hurry up, we're going to be late!" Our first nerve was pinched. They were three hours late to pick us up and pulled up hollering at us. We got our last kisses and hugs from those there to see us off as we loaded our luggage and at 11:15am we were off. Ghana here we come!

Our flight was leaving at 3:30 pm but we need to check in early. My son and his friend Tony were driving following behind the van to see us off at the airport. We took route 295 to 95 at exit 7a at 12:25 pm in New Jersey when the driver pulled in to a rest stop to have the brake fluid checked. The driver said the brakes were soft. He called dispatch to ask for another van to come and continue the trip for us.

I immediately understood exactly why John and I were led to travel a day earlier and spend the night at an airport hotel and we are now very sorry we hadn't yielded to the leading of Spirit. Tony said that he would leave the others and take John and I on to the airport and I wish we had gone on ahead but we didn't leave them. We waited with the others and the replacement vehicle arrived at 1:50 pm, we transferred the luggage but the traffic didn't allow us to make up for the lost time.

We arrived at the airport at 3:35 pm watching our plane flying off over our heads. We found out those in the group who were on a different van were on the plane but Ted was there with our tickets and passports. The airline wasn't required to give us any lodging because our missing the flight was not their fault.

Ted shook his head like he couldn't believe what happened. He said he was confused when two vans showed up that morning and he sent one away and hours later had to re-order the same van to come for us. We told him to try for some type of solution. He tried to negotiate our tickets with another airline to no avail because the tickets weren't endorsed. The shuttle service wanted to return half our transport money or take us back home.

It was no way we were going back home. "Forward ever backward never." as Kwame Nkrumah made the statement famous. We were adamant and not going back to Philadelphia.

After we sat around the airport for hours trying to decide what to do, John and I stored our 16 boxes of luggage at the airport for $198.00 and headed for the Holiday Inn at $149.00 a night. We were rescheduled to travel the next Tuesday at 10pm on Ghana Airways. I was so disappointed I couldn't speak. We weren't having charitable feelings for anyone responsible for making us miss our flight.

My son and Tony assisted them by transporting Rita and their luggage from the airport to Harlem. Rita was taking them to a cousin's house where they could all stay together. The luggage was so much that Ted and Donna couldn't fit in the car and had to take the subway.

Latif and Tony reported carrying the luggage up to a third floor apartment for Ted who didn't help at all but gave them $10.00 to share and told them the kids in Ghana will appreciate what they've done for them. We saw this as the second time it appeared our dream may not come true. John took it well and said we were only delayed, we will reach our destination, don't you worry babe, as he hugged me tight.

He said we'd better inform Ann who was going to meet us at Kotoka Airport in Ghana that we've missed our flight. When I called her she said it was just in time because she had gone to the car to leave Cape Coast to travel three to four hours to Accra to meet us, and returned to the house to answer the phone. If the call had come through a minute later she would have driven off, it was 4:30 am in Ghana.

When we listen to the promptings of the Holy Spirit telling us to do the right thing at the right time we can't go wrong. Things will be done decently and in order when we obey promptly. Most of the time there's too much interference crowding out the still small voice of reason. We don't listen and later say Oh I should have followed my first mind.

The Lord could see ahead that we were going to miss our plane if we didn't stay overnight at an airport hotel. We didn't insist on doing what we knew was right for us. John and I knew what we were supposed to do, but we gave in to the group leader and didn't follow the one who leads our lives. Now we were paying the price for not obeying. So we accepted the consequences of our actions and moved on to learn from our mistakes.

We made the best of the Holiday Inn for Saturday, Sunday and Monday nights, we had fun watching the planes taking off and prayed to be on the Tuesday night 10pm Ghana Airway flight.

My son and Tony stayed overnight at the hotel but had to get back to Philly the next day. It was very hard to part with my son. Yet I felt the distance would be good for the both of us in the long run. It's been just the two of us since he was two years old; now the umbilical cord had to be cut again at age 21. We both shed tears and embraced while I prayed all would be well with him as he found his way through life. I'd only be a phone call or email away to reach out to communicate with him anytime. I felt like I was being torn apart but I had to go to Afrika. This pull on my heart was stronger than the bonds of motherhood that would keep me in America. We offered Latif the opportunity to come with us but he declined.

All our clothes were in storage so we had to shop for something to wear for our extended days. We met Andrea who worked in reservations at the hotel. She was so excited about our trip especially when we told her it was John's first flight at his age, and how we were going for the first time and not returning to America. She introduced us to a couple of the Ghana Airway pilots who were also lodging at the hotel and they said they'd invite us up to the cockpit on our way to Ghana.

Everyone who heard about us got so excited and commented on our courage. We were just going home. Andrea wrote the names and phone numbers of her friends in Ghana and told us to look them up. She visited Ghana many times before and told us some dos and don'ts like you can eat Shitto but don't eat grass-cutter. The name Shitto doesn't sound good but it's a pepper sauce. A bush rodent that only eats grass is considered a delicacy by some Ghanaians called the grass-cutter and is sort of like the muskrat we know. She also told us to go to the W.E.B. Dubois Center to look for friends of hers and wrote a note in our book for them to take good care of us, her new family. We appreciated her contacts and words of wisdom.

It was July 6th, 1999 and we were at the airport early for check-in. Ghana Airway terminal was congested! I've never seen such chaos! There was no queue. It seemed that we were on standby and not even sure if we were scheduled for the flight. People were pushing and shoving, emptying suitcases and rearranging their belongings. We couldn't get any information and I became caught up in the confusion. I became worried and pushed and shoved back because I wanted to be on the plane that night! We must be on the plane to Ghana! I felt as though I was fighting for my survival, for my life! Why was there so much commotion to board an air flight? After we talked to this person and that person, finally our tickets were processed and we were led to the waiting area, but I couldn't relax until I was sitting in the plane seat. John appeared cool and reassured me that all was well, but he was chain smoking at the same time which didn't give me confidence.

When they started calling seat numbers to embark the passengers were still rather unruly, as if someone else can sit in their assigned seat. At last John and I took the walk onto the plane and down the aisle. One of the ladies in the group was bumped up to first class, and good for her, I was just elated to be in the number of folks on the plane to Ghana.

Mother-Father Creator, forgive me for doubting. I wish I could have kept my peace and not forgotten you are in control of all that concerns John and I. You have begun a good work in us and surely you will bring it to completion. Help us to be anxious for nothing and in all our ways to honor you and let you direct our path. So be it!

I love taking off in an airplane, all except for the popping in the ears. The stewardesses were pleasant and two of the pilots we met at the Holiday Inn were flying. John's seat was in front of mine and I kept asking him how he was faring. He was happy as a result of tasting Ghana's famous Star Beer and was not a bit anxious. Midway into the flight the pilots sent for us to come up to the cockpit and join them. Can you believe it! John and I were sitting up there watching all those controls, and drinking juice with them while flying through the clouds.

The Captain announced we were flying over 600 miles per hour at an altitude of 3,900 hundred feet. This could never be allowed in this present day and age of airline security. We seemed to be such a phenomenon to everyone who heard our story and the pilots commented over and over of our courage to pack up and travel to Ghana to stay the way we were doing. The ride was so smooth and it never seemed that we traveled for nine hours. We touched down in Dakar to refuel but we didn't get off the plane. The next thing we saw was AKWAABA! Welcome to KOTOKA INTERNATIONAL AIRPORT! We landed softly. The pilots of Ghana Airways were very capable and it is unfortunate that *Ghana Airways* is not in operation today. It is no longer in operation.

Bringing the gifts that my ancestors gave,
I am the dream and the hope of the slave.
I rise, I rise, I rise!
Maya Angelou

13

Dear Ancestors We Are Home

What a mighty God we serve! I still wouldn't believe I was on Afrikas' soil until my feet were off the plane and on the ground. It was all so surreal and John and I kept pinching each other and asked had we truly arrived in Afrika? Every one moved at a fast pace and I could hardly keep up while picking up our luggage and going through customs. We had no problem with Ted leading the way and were in and out speedily. We looked for Ann who was to meet us and take most of our luggage to her house in Cape Coast. We asked her to do this because we didn't want to carry sixteen boxes around while going travelling with the group.

We were scheduled to stay in Ghana for ten days, and travel to South Africa for one week. The group would return to Ghana for five more days and leave for America while John and I would remain in Accra, Ghana. Once we've found a place to reside we'd pick up the baggage from her. We heard Ann calling hello John and Joann. We knew her from seeing the videos and we previously mailed her pictures of ourselves. We hugged her and thanked her for assisting us but we only had time to transfer the boxes into her truck and return to the group.

We didn't kiss the ground but oh how glad we were to finally be in Ghana! Our eyes were as big as saucers trying to take everything in.

Downtown Accra is a modern city full of tall buildings and nice roads. The traffic was heavy and chaotic, horns were blowing loudly and some people sported the latest auto models such as Mercedes, Lexus and Land Rovers.

We passed an area that looked like a gigantic open air market place and was very crowded. The people moved fast, women carried heaps of parcels on their heads with babies on their backs and didn't miss a step. I sensed a rhythm in all the movement.

There were various dialects and the voices were loud. The sun was hot! Ghana is parallel to the equator we learned during our research, but the sun was feeling good on my skin. You could appreciate it when a cool breeze blew by. The smells were pungent, musky, and fruity to name a few. The dirt was red clay color. Everything looked so colorful! A Muslim call to prayer could be heard above the crowd. I observed so much character in the faces of many elders.

The driver that met us was named Joseph. I wondered what the Afrikan name his mother gave him was but I kept that thought to myself. We arrived at an area called Mamprobi a suburb of Accra, when Ted said we had to stop to visit the tribal chief of the village and let him know we were in town. We sat in a circle and everyone shook hands, we were welcomed and someone had to interpret what the chief said to us and in turn what we said to him. The visit was short but seemed to be a necessary custom to be fulfilled.

We were taken to DeLuxe Hotel in Accra. Since we didn't know what to expect John and I thought the place was adequate. Somehow it looked like maybe it had been closed down but re-opened just for our group. I had difficulty managing the stairs to the second floor but persevered. Our modest room was dimly lit with old furniture but had a veranda where we could look out over the vicinity. We dropped our bags and stepped out onto the balcony, kissed, squeezed each other tight and praised God for bringing us this far by faith. The date was the 7th of July, 1999.

At last we were home! We have returned ourselves who were stolen from the motherland. John and I were in the bowels of our ancestors, and were brought forth in America. We come from a people who had no choice and weren't invited to America but were captured, shackled, starved, whipped, raped, murdered and enslaved during the Trans Atlantic Slave Trade. We are of those who were stripped of almost everything. The cruelest of all was not to be able to keep our own culture, our native tongue, our own names, or our own religion. Our captors didn't even want us to learn how to read or write; they didn't want us to play our drums, or sing our own songs. Spirit of our ancestors we are here.

Dear ancestors, we've heard your pleas . . . we've heard your cries . . . we've answered your call. We have remembered. We have come home. Our feet are on the Continent of Mother Afrika, where we belong. We gave thanks!

This part of town in Accra reminded me of home in North Philly we were used to which some would call the ghetto, where people are real and down to earth. We felt at home immediately. I called my sister Nia in Philadelphia to tell her we had touched down safely. She asked me how is it over there in Afrika? I told her it reminded me of one big flea market inside a modern city and feels like home. There was no order to the way the houses were built, some were frontward, backward, sideways and high class expensive homes were next to lower income homes, mud houses, and thatched roofs and kiosks were all mixed together. I told her I'd tell her more at another time.

Meanwhile some in the group were talking about going to shop for material. Others said they would cook dinner then later said we'd all go out for dinner. Those who had been to Ghana before joined cliques, so we told them when they decided what to do to let us know. When they organized themselves they took us to a nice place to have dinner. The menu had Jamaican-Caribbean and Ghanaian dishes and the food was good.

The restaurant was on the second floor so I had a bit of a struggle but managed. The terrain was uneven and rocky, it's dark and I used a cane, I had to walk slow and watch my step very well. As we joined the van to return to the hotel the members of the group arranged themselves in such a way that John and I couldn't sit next to each other as we did going to dinner. John asked them to rearrange themselves so that we could, but no one would mind him. When John said to me let's take a taxi back to the hotel Ted says he wouldn't recommend it this time of night. He said we were in a part of town which was considered dangerous.

It was about midnight and we didn't even know where we were. Instead of the group leaders asking their folks to accommodate us by allowing us to sit together, no one paid us any attention. I asked my husband to just take the available seats so we could go. He sat in back while I was in the front. He was so upset with me for giving in to this situation. It was the source of our first argument our first night in Ghana.

This was the third strike for these folks as far as I was concerned. If they had no respect for us as a couple and further for my husband as an elder, then for sure we were with the wrong group of people. I had to assure John that I didn't acquiesce to the group because I agreed with them. I had decided that I wouldn't step in that van to go anywhere with them again. They would not get another chance to treat us disrespectfully again.

So the next day when the group was deciding what activities to do for the day we told them we weren't interested and we would not be traveling with them again. Sometimes when people kick you, they kick you forward. The maltreatment shown to us by the group forced John and I to begin adventuring out on our own as a couple.

Denkyem (Adinkra symbol of adaptability)
Denkyem da nsuo mu, nso nnhome nsuo ohome mframa
The crocodile lives in water but it does not breathe water,
It breathes air.
Meaning: It encourages people to conform to the way of life
Of people among which they find themselves

14

Checking Out Accra, The Capital

John and I started taking in the sights of the immediate area and were on our own ever since. We found a place to have our breakfast egg, toast and coffee. It was so funny how they chopped the scrambled eggs up in tiny pieces.

The first thing we needed to do was find a Barclays Bank to deposit our money. We had chosen this bank before our arrival because we could have a dollar account and wire transfers. We were rushed out of the airport following the group and never stopped at the window to declare the money we had in our possession. We each had money strapped to our thighs while flying here and as we moved around town. It was a good thing we had the letter from the lawyer to prove how the money came into our possession and we opened a bank account immediately.

We rode around in taxi's sightseeing and eventually met some people in close proximity to the hotel. We befriended a young man named George who owned a barbershop with a communication center inside where we made our phone calls. He was a small businessman and his character seemed good.

John and I asked George to take us around Makola Market (An open commercial area of several hundred acres.); we purchased a small stereo, some Ghanaian music CD's, a few clothes, and a percolator so we could make our coffee in the hotel room. We bought a mobile phone from Ghana Telecom. We tried various neighborhood restaurants and took our time taking chances with different foods. We ate spaghetti, chicken and fried rice for awhile and slowly eased into the Ghanaian cuisine.

On our third day in Ghana we heeded the airline Captains' advice and looked at properties around Legon another suburb of Accra. We would ride around looking until we'd see a sale or lease sign on a house and if the caretaker was in they'd show the house. The homes in this area were elegant and even lavish and you couldn't help but like them but they looked like presidential palaces. They were much too grand for our taste.

We knew living this kind of lifestyle would bring us to financial ruin quickly. The first house was called an Executive Estate and leased for 7,200,000.00 Ghana Cedis a month which equaled $2,880.00 U.S. dollars. At the same time people in America are wondering if people in Afrika live in houses. The next house was more lavish at $3,000.00 a month to lease. These houses were fenced in gated compounds with marbled floors and columns, five bedrooms, two-car garages, with large patios.

We soon saw that we needed to keep doing our research because we did not want to live the lifestyle of the rich and famous. However it was an education to see the various economic levels from the lowest to the highest. We had only seen a glimpse of the high end bracket, there was much more to see. We would later meet Rose and Albie Walls who live on the boarder of Trasacco Valley Housing Development where the homes range from $700,000.00 to over a million dollars to purchase.

The next few days we hired a taxi by the day (eight hours) for twenty-five Ghana Cedis and began our search around Achimota, Madina, and Dansoman, more suburbs of Accra and found a couple of homes that we liked. Now finding the owners of the properties was another story. When we were trying to find a certain place and stop to ask directions from someone; they would say "let me show you" and jump in the car with us to take us directly to the place we were looking for. The driver told us to dash them some small money for their time.

We'd meet people for the very first time and they'd say "I want to be your friend or now you are my friend." This could possibly be because we're foreigners and new to the country or they could smell money. This is different from our culture on the other side where "friend" means someone you have known and trust for a good number of years.

In Dansoman, Accra we found homes of more moderate prices from 300.00 to 800,000.00 Ghana Cedis to lease a month. These houses were smaller but nice gated compounds with 3 bedrooms and nicely landscaped. Only outside the compound the community environment was filled with loud music and trash heaps. We saw a billboard picture of a huge cat advertising cat stew, and we said what another person eats doesn't make us fat. Although it did make us leery of eating any stews of which we couldn't identify the meat.

John and I could see that Accra was such a large metropolis, crowded with people, traffic logged, with sanitation problems and probably many transients moved to the big city from the rural areas looking for jobs and a better life. Too many people were walking the streets through the traffic selling various items and numerous physically challenged people in wheelchairs or on rolling boards would come to car windows begging for alms.

We found one house we liked which was in the care of the owner's lawyer but we couldn't locate him. Accra is such a large fast paced crowded city which reminded us of New York, and before we arrived we thought we'd live in Accra. Both of us soon had second thoughts but we did have to find another place to live besides the hotel we were in. John thought it better if we leave the hotel and lease a place temporarily while we looked for a permanent place to settle down.

We called Ann to tell her what we were doing. She begged us not to give money to anyone, maybe fearing we might be duped. Then she said why don't you come and see Cape Coast? You might like it. What is stopping you? John said nothing, we'll come tomorrow. She told us to take the STC bus to Cape Coast and take a taxi from the bus stop to Fairhill Guesthouse.

"Sing me your folk songs and
I'll tell you about the character,
Custom's and history of your people"
Paul Robeson

15

Why Don't You Come To Cape Coast?

Ted asked us if we were going on to South Afrika with them and of course we were not. I overheard him saying to other group members that they couldn't reach the Dr. whom they were planning to reside with-in Jo'berg. However they were still going and that sometimes they'd bunk out at people's homes and make a pallet on the floor. That was not the way we wanted to travel. I still have the airline tickets in my possession. The tickets for South Afrika are along with the return tickets to America. We wished them well and told him we were going to visit Ann in Cape Coast. Ann had stopped her busy schedule to be of assistance to us and never mentioned that her mother was critically ill, and now her mother had passed away, we were going to be with her.

We left all our worldly goods locked in the hotel room and took enough clothes to stay with Ann a couple of days. The STC bus station was crowded; we bought our tickets at a nominal price and waited, and waited, and waited.

My first culture shock was when I asked for a ladies room and was showed a place called a female urinal which was just a gutter to squat over. Then I found they did have a toilet but that is if you have to do more than urinate. You pay a small fee and they give you some T-roll (toilet tissue). So be specific when asking for the ladies room.

It was four hours before we boarded the bus with not even an explanation or an apology for the delay. Although we all had tickets with seat numbers, people began to push and shove to get on the bus just like they did at the airport. I was disturbed because we were leaving Accra at the time we were expected to be in Cape Coast. Everybody around us seemed to take this like it was normal. So as "when in Rome", I chilled myself out and enjoyed the ride.

The STC or State Transport Company bus was like a Greyhound bus that we know in the USA and was comfortable. The scenery once outside Accra was more and more luscious green hills, valleys, savannahs, farmland, forest, large ant hills, and villages with luxury homes blended between modest homes and huts. Me and my naiveté, I was sure I'd see wild animals running through the plains, but all I saw were goats, cows, chickens, cats and dogs roaming.

The ride to Cape Coast took another three hours and we had a good nap on the way. I woke up just in time to see the ocean and palm trees along the coast, how lovely it was with many fishing boats sailing and I could see fishermen pulling in their nets. I vowed to one day help to pull in one of those fish nets. I love seafood so much that I may be from a fishing village. We read that Cape Coast and Elmina's main industry was from fishing.

There were wood carvers working on huge long pieces of wood like long oak trees making boats. Market ladies at their stands with their oranges and tomatoes stacked like pyramids, beautiful sights along the way.

It was Monday 12th July, 1999 when we arrived at Fairhill Guesthouse. Ann was so warm and welcoming. We entered our room and we were astonished at the difference between her hotel and the one we were staying in; it was literally night and day. The room was bright, with modern furniture, a king-size bed, TV, VCR and a mini refrigerator with drinks and snacks inside. John is thinking what I'm thinking that we were definitely staying at the wrong hotel and we should be staying here.

When we ate the food it was just like being on the other side. We could see how the USA had rubbed off on Ann. We would come to find out that she lived and worked in America over twenty years and she brought some of the good ideas back with her. We met Ricky, Ann's husband whom we had spoken to over the phone previously and these two made a nice couple.

Ann took us to her family house where all her family was gathered because her mother had passed just the day before. The entire family greeted us as we all sat in a circle. There was a lot of hand shaking from right to left and plenty of expressions of affection shown. Ann's brother and family head (Ebusuapanyin) Emanuel, her elder sister Agnes, Aunt Araba, Leticia and Elizabeth other family and friends were so kind.

There was a naming ceremony planned for us. In Fante culture you have a name given to you by the day of the week that you are born and this is how John became Kofi and I became Adjoa. Ye frem me (my name is) Adjoa Abaka Abanyie aka Adjoa Childs. This tells you I'm born on Monday and I'm the first born in my family. Abanyie is the name of our adopted Ghanaian family. I like the name Pa Kofi Esoun Abanyie Panyin much better for John. This means he's born on a Friday, the 7th born in his family and a wise elder.

This is according to the Fante clan in Cape Coast, Ghana. I will call him John or Kofi interchangeably throughout this book. At the time we didn't know the exact day of our birth because in America we only celebrate the date and not the day but these names we felt were fitting for us so we adopted them.

We visited friends of Ann's named Ato and Ivy Cobbina who lived in a dream house on a hill with a view of the ocean. Ato is a dentist who once practiced in West Philadelphia many years and has now returned home to Ghana with offices in Cape Coast and Accra, Ivy worked for Peace Corps. What a small world; we met another friend of Ann's named John a Ghanaian who had been a policeman in our same city of Philadelphia and recently retired. Ann was instrumental in urging Ato and John to return home and invest as she had.

We could see the Creator put us in the hands of a very dynamic lady in the person of Mrs. Anastasia Hooper. We liked Cape Coast because we could see the ocean as we drove around parts of the town. This was a quaint smaller town and not as congested as Accra. We loved Ann and everyone we met in her circle so far and it was only the first day. We decided to send her driver to the hotel in Accra the next day to bring all our belongings to Fairhill Guesthouse in Cape Coast.

The next day eight in the morning Ann was ready to take on the day and she got us up and out immediately after breakfast. We visited Ann and

Ricky's home and their hotel annex, the main central general hospital, Dr. Cobbina's Stovie Dental clinic and Auntie Gladys with her big smile from Detroit who ran a medical clinic.

Ann showed us an uncompleted house to see if we were interested to move into. She thought I might like it because when the high grass was cut it had a view of a lagoon. By now I had told everyone I wanted a house by the ocean. John said he could envision the place completed but we had only seen the outside of the house and I wasn't convinced. I had never thought of completing someone else's house to live in and rent but I opened up to the suggestion.

We're being spoiled and well taken care of at Fairhill Guesthouse yet we knew we couldn't stay there forever. Ann packed a lot into a day and all the above was accomplished just before noon. At lunchtime we met about a dozen members of Rickey Hooper's family who had gathered at the guesthouse in support of Ann's' mothers' funeral. They were all very friendly and it was a lot of names to try to remember but Alberta and Ebow stood out.

Ann dropped us off at the Cape Coast Castle and returned to pick us up a few hours later. Castle is a dressed up name for a dungeon, a slave castle where our ancestors were kept captive before boarding the slave ship through the door of no return for the Middle Passage. The outside is white-washed and the inside is dreary. A film was shown as soon as we entered and it gave some history linking Continental mainland Afrikans to Afrikans in the Diaspora.

We were shown around to the male and female quarters' which were small, dark and musty. You could imagine our ancestors crowded in there with no fresh air, 1000 men in one room and 500 women in another, no light, chained together, no toilet, and fed gruel just enough to keep them alive. When you inhaled you smelled the blood, the sweat, felt the grime on the floor and the walls from centuries ago and imagined their groans, their cries and their prayers. Then we saw the door of no return where our ancestors left, never to return again.

We went to the captain's quarters near the chapel and saw the entrance where they slipped our mothers, aunties, sisters and nieces in and out of the captain's quarters. Can you believe there was a church in this wretched place! I prayed to myself to keep from slipping into a deep depression. Kofi had tears in his eyes.

I communed with the ancestors. I felt a praise rising from deep in my spirit. I sensed that those who had gone on before us were happy that we returned to Afrika. A surge of dominion, dignity and release flooded my soul; Yes! It's alright now. They took you over the Atlantic Ocean in chains without your permission but we have paid for our tickets, paid the ransom and come home.

Now from the door of no return there is a door of return! We honor you dear ancestors and the Afrikan Holy Ghost who has sustained our people since the beginning of time.

We honor each and every man, woman, boy and girl who made the Atlantic Ocean their grave along that treacherous journey. We remember the price you paid so that we could live free. We are from you and you are in us and we are a great people! Our greatness will manifest again.

We will have to once again show the world that we Afrikans' put the "civil" in civilization as John Henry Clarke said. Oh Yes! It's alright now. We didn't forget you. We will never forget you. We have come, and our bones will be buried here. We thank you for calling us home and we are glad to be counted worthy to be home. Praises to the Creator of the universe!

We couldn't go anywhere else after that experience. I liken it to making the Hajj and definitely one pilgrimage recommended to every Afrikan in the Diaspora to experience at least once in their lifetime. Just to have a glimpse of what the people whose shoulders we stand on went through.

We read that most of the slave castles, forts, and slave trading posts are located in Ghana, which was another one of our reasons for choosing to resettle here. We felt this to be holy ground. We went back to the hotel to rest and it was hard to put our experience into words. We went into deep reflection and found ourselves in need of quiet time. It's also good to sit by the ocean after visiting the slave dungeons to cleanse your aura.

"I live in Ghana; I don't just
Visit or vacation here"
In Ghana Here
Rose Jones Walls

16

Settling Down In Aquarium Down

Every morning eight a.m. we'd hear Ann's car horn beep upon her arrival
to the hotel. We loved how she'd come in our room and round us up for
the day's activities as we were having breakfast. This day we were supposed
to visit Elmina Slave Castle. However this particular morning she found us
both in bed feverish, and hardly able to lift our heads. The more she tried
to get us to get up and get going we replied we could not go anywhere to
do anything. She then said oh dear don't tell me, malaria?

We didn't have any warning symptoms, and felt as if we had the flu.
We had muscle aches and intermittent chills and just wanted to sleep. She
purchased some medicine and we took it and rested for two days before
we felt like exploring Cape Coast again. I wondered if the visit to the Slave
Castle was so shocking to our system that we allowed it to make us sick.
We sure felt fine until we went there. We had no signs of illness prior.

I couldn't help Kofi and he couldn't help me because we were both
sick at the same time once again. This is too much togetherness for me.
We were probably just run down after all the excitement, the stress of
preparing to come to Ghana; and our arrival at last surely must have taken
a toll on our physical and emotional systems.

So taking the preventive medicine for two weeks prior and once a week after arriving in Ghana didn't prevent us from getting malaria, but protected us from getting a severe case of it. You have to keep your immune system built up, and you have to know your body system.

Please don't let fear of getting malaria keep you from visiting Afrika because when you take the medicine in time you get over it quickly. It felt like the normal cold and flu we would often catch in the wintertime in America. It is proper to get a lab test to verify that malaria parasites have been cleared from the bloodstream.

Ann took us to Afrikan Americans who were living in Iture, Elmina to meet Mr. and Mrs.Okofu of One Afrika Guesthouse. Ted also mentioned them in America before the trip because of their beautiful ocean front property. We met Nana Ben who was made an Asafo Chief (head of the male military group) in his town and his Queen Imakus. Both of them adorned with long mixed gray locks of hair and appearing very blessed to be living in Ghana.

We put our hands out to shake and Nana said "you've come too far for a handshake" and gave us both a big strong embrace. He and Imakus went on to tell us some of their trials and tribulations; although not to discourage us but to forewarn us of some things. They especially said to buy some land and put down some roots and build, but be very careful dealing with people; and said that Ann should lead us around when we were ready.

Down the road we went to meet Rabbi Kohain at Mable's Table Restaurant. This was another lovely ocean front place to sit and enjoy a fantastic ocean view with Elmina Slave Castle in the distance. Kohain's a charismatic and knowledgeable young man who is a leader of one of the Hebrew Israelite groups in the area. He welcomed us wholeheartedly and his wife Mable a beautiful Ghanaian lady too busy to socialize because she was busy in the kitchen.

I said a silent prayer of thanks to the Almighty for the piece of ocean front land he had in store for us. We were very glad to know where to locate others from "our clan" of Afrikans from America.

Ann put us on a bus to Tema for a weekend visit to her sister Aggie and her husband Nana Edmond Brakohiapa. We were in awe and felt we were in a royal palace. Her husband is a chief from his home town Kyebi. There was a picture of him in his full regalia of gold and Kente cloth. The home was so spacious and pristine, while Aggie and Nana were warm and humble.

They made us feel so welcome that we felt we were staying in a five star hotel. A friend of theirs who dropped in named Kojo Blankston told us many stories about tradition and of him being the head of his tribal military company. The funniest story he told was how we are all like lizards holding on to the globe and at times some of us get tired and fall off. (May his soul now rest in perfect peace.)

Once back in Cape Coast Kofi and I were able to go look at the unfinished house with Ann and Aggie and the three of them sold me on it and Ann pushed because it was now a month that we stayed in her hotel; she felt that enough time and money had been spent and we needed a permanent residence. It was said the house sat unfinished for seven years. Kofi loved a good challenge and promised me once the plaster, painting, plumbing and electricity was complete, that I would love the house.

I guess I just wanted to move into a completely finished place but I'm up for the adventure. We paid the lump sum of $220.00 a month for a two year lease to the landlord with Ann as a witness for him to use the money to complete the house. He didn't speak English and we didn't understand Fante so she had to interpret for the both of us. This was a five bedroom house with three baths, with front and back veranda's but not a fenced compound.

Ann found someone to weed the high grass so we could see the lagoon. We didn't have to worry about anything except for the landlord to have the work completed in two-three weeks time. Ann moved like a lightening rod always taking us by the house to check on the progress and push the laborers to work well and fast. Kofi tried to offer incentives like buying crates of minerals (sodas) and we had each bought one hundred dollars of $2.00 bills to hand out as tips.

However Ghanaian business people told us to stop tipping like that because we would spoil the market. We were very freely handing out those two dollar bills, to waiters and waitresses and we were so happy to do it. Looking back I guess it looked rather foolish to be new in the town behaving like money grew on trees.

We saw our motives were misconstrued, not seen as generosity from the heart but as weakness and stupidity. Ann purchased the $2.00 bills from us to dissuade us from giving them out further. The two dollars were equal to five Ghana Cedis. The normal rate to tip a person was one or two Ghana Cedis not two dollars.

Two and half weeks have passed and the minor details that have to be finished can be done even while we're living in the house though the list is long. We've applied to the Electricity Company of Ghana for service and it's connected. Ghana Telecom has charged us for two poles and the wire to get our phone lines up and running.

We have acquired our postal box and all this is thanks to Ann going back and forth with us several times to literally beg for the services and then give a dash for the service to be provided. A dash we would learn is financial motivation for getting services completed. However Kofi and I weren't used to tipping people until and unless they've done a good job for us.

We are not at all used to giving government workers money to do their jobs. Later when we would find ourselves going in circles or going back and forth and up and down trying to get things accomplished we would finally understand we hadn't played by the rules and were paying the price.

Ann took us to carpenters to have a living room and dining room set made, a king sized bed for our bedroom, and three queen sized beds made for the guestrooms. We wanted to have Ghana made furniture for our home although there were stores that sold imported modern styles. Then we needed an entertainment center to place our television and stereo on in the living room. This transaction turned out to be entertainment in itself.

When the carpenters delivered the set to our house, they entered with one large piece, another large piece and then an additional large piece of furniture to connect together. What in the world is it and where can we put it I asked? Meanwhile Ann can't stop laughing because the set is so long it's blocking the doorway. If we turn it to another wall we can't see out the windows. Kofi was shaking his head saying he should have been more specific on the measurements or should have drawn a picture for them because this is definitely not what we were expecting. It was so big, bulky and long.

Ann's laughter was so infectious we all ended up laughing, even the carpenters. Thankfully we had a pantry that was very long and we could put the "entertainment center" in there where it could be useful for dishes, canned goods and other storage items. We would soon find that laughter would be the best response to many frustrating situations that would come our way.

Our luggage and boxes were taken to the new house at Aquarium Down, and Ann took us to our new home. How happy we were! She did so much for us and at last we were settled in the house we would call home for the next two years. We couldn't have done it without her assistance and drive.

We've purchased a refrigerator, stove, dishes, utensils, glasses, iron and board, and pots and pans. We were in Ghana less than two months and we had a place to lay our heads. Praise God! Ann, Kofi and I planned so well that all the furniture was ready and in the house before we moved in.

Our first night getting to know our semi-permanent home; I stepped in the shower to bathe, placed my hand on the handle to turn on the water and I got shocked. I stepped out the tub and tried again, shocked! What in the world is going on here, and I screamed for Kofi, help! He checked it out and it happened to him too. So we just washed up at the face bowl and called it a night.

However when we reported it to the landlord he checked for the electrical earth rod and found it was not dug deep enough into the ground and had it fixed. I was skeptical of touching the faucet again but happily no more shocks.

The landlord came back to us saying he needed more money to finish the work in the house so we gave him six additional months of rent money. This now gave us two and half years to be in his house. One down side to this is during the process of moving our possessions either from Accra to Cape Coast or within Cape Coast we lost some important papers and all of Kofi's collection of jazz music discs. I was heartbroken for him but he rebounded fast not being too tied down to material things.

Since we had all the donated school supplies Kofi and I thought it a good way to meet the neighbors by going round our immediate vicinity and give items to the children. So we did and were graciously accepted by Ghanaians in every house that we visited. We learned some of the names of the neighbors and when we sat on our porch we could wave and speak as they passed by daily.

Our neighbors immediately across from us were very congenial and helpful. Ama and John were grandparents to Adwoa (pronounced Adjoa like my name), Ato, Kwesie, Abeku and Baba. They offered to teach us fante and some culture. Ato and Abeku were carpenters, Kwesie was a mason and Adwoa owned a hair salon. We could call on them anytime we had questions. Ato's wife made the curtains for our house and baked nice cakes that we enjoyed.

There were government workers, businessmen and women in this community, many teachers, a chop bar (small eating and drinking spot), a fitter (car mechanic), and a very loud church. The frogs sang out every night because we were near the lagoon and it sounded like hundreds in my imagination. We soon became accustomed to our environment and we could begin to settle down and enjoy our little piece of Cape Coast, Ghana.

Ann drove us to her hometown of Odonase where her parents lived before her father moved to Cape Coast. We met the chief of the town and told him we'd return with items donated to give to the school. We were given a date to return and a list of additional items that the school needed.

When we returned to the village there was a large durbar prepared for our arrival. This area was set aside for the town people to witness activities pertinent to their village. They set up tents in a large squared area to keep the sun off the crowd and hundreds of plastic chairs. Chairs for us, the chief, and his entourage were set up on a podium.

We surely didn't expect all the fanfare but this was how it's done in Ghana. Activates should be transparent for all to see what was given and who received the donations. We had desks and chairs and cabinets made by carpenters, bought a bicycle, clocks, and a seamstress made a dozen uniforms for boys and girls.

The names of the neediest children were called to come to receive their gifts. There were plenty of books, pens, pencils, tablets, crayons, rulers, given to us to circulate by friends who brought them to our going away party for charity. There was also a cash donation of $250.00 and everyone was so appreciative. It was a great day and so fulfilling for us as givers as well as for the receivers.

The next week it was time to visit Auntie Gladys Rice at Kwapro Clinic, built by her church in Michigan-Fellowship Chapel, located on the campus of Cape Coast University with the medical supplies we were given to distribute. The clinic was known to be very helpful in the community especially for the treatment of malaria in young children and pregnant mothers. We were able to give such items as medicines, alcohol, iodine, bandages, gauze, ointments, syringes, tooth brushes, toothpaste and such which would surely be put to good use.

When we went to Zion School where Aunt Araba teaches, we were swarmed with a crowd of beautiful smiling children so anxious to thank us for the few things we had to offer to the school. The songs they sang brought tears to our eyes, their voices were so melodious. No one sings like an Afrikan, their voices are very distinctive and soulful. Beautiful! Yes it is better to give than to receive.

I wrote a newsletter about our trip thus far and titled it Dreams Do Come True. I sent it to family and friends back in the states and got no response at all. We contacted an internet provider for service at home and tried it out for $25.00 a month. Oh but the speed was slower than a snail and would hardly download anything.

I grew tired of paying and waiting for internet service and discontinued it after about six months. I could never accomplish anything over the web and could barely send an email. So it was less expensive to use the E-cafes around town. Even today ten years later there is little improvement in the speed of the computer service in the area I now live. Technological assistance is much need here.

Kofi and I gave ourselves a birthday party which also served as an open house; and invited all the new folks we met in Cape Coast. We invited all the people who were instrumental in helping us get settled in our new place of residence; all the laborers, artisans, businessmen and women friends and family. But we noticed that the laborers, artisans and workers automatically separated themselves from the businessmen and women and wouldn't mix with us and our family and friends. They moved themselves off to another area of the house. We asked them why and were told although the working class and the middle class are friendly they would never socialize together. This was how we found out about a class system that is entrenched in Ghana.

"God bless the child that's got his own."
Billie Holiday

Handling Our Business

My dear Kofi disliked taking taxis to get around so we solicited the help of Prof. Fifi a lecturer at Cape Coast University and his friend Chairman to take us to Kumasi to buy a vehicle. We met Fifi (another name for Kofi) at Barclays Bank and Chairman was a spray painter of vehicles and a driver at Siwdo, a large open area garage where vehicles are repaired.

We went on our adventure to see another part of Ghana and prayed to return with our own car or truck. At lunchtime our friends had a place they liked to stop where they could get grass-cutter they liked. I lost my appetite watching them sucking the meat out the head of that animal. Kofi asked for the heads when they were finished. He would later sterilize them and keep them in a glass for a souvenir. I don't have any idea why.

Kumasi was a four hour drive from Cape Coast and once there we had to first stop at Fifis' family house because he said he had to let them know he was in town. He said you can never let it be said that you came into your hometown and didn't stop at the family house before you made your rounds around town. His family all gathered to greet us like we were long lost family members and said they'd give us land in the area if we wanted it. We were finding out that "give you" really meant sell you. We begged permission to leave, it was granted and we said our goodbyes.

Kumasi is a modern beautifully planned city and the landscape is of luscious green foliage and is rightly named the "Garden City." We went round and round, up and down looking and pricing trucks. It appeared we were going home empty handed when Kofi spotted a red truck up on a hill and he shouted "make a U turn quick!"

He inspected the truck and haggled with the price a bit and decided on it even though it had manual drive. He hadn't driven one in fifty years but he said it's just like riding a bike, you never forget. Never mind that I couldn't drive a clutch, Kofi said I had him to drive me around.

We found a Barclays Bank, made a withdrawal and walked out with a shopping bag full of money because the denominations were small. Chairman and Fifi protected us like armed guard security men out of the bank to the car and back to the used car dealer. Every dollar was equivalent to 2,500.00 Ghana Cedis at the time. We paid 17,500.00 Ghana Cedis which was $7,000.00 in dollars. The only hitch it was dark and certain paperwork had to be completed the next day. We had to find a hotel and stay overnight while our friends stayed at Fifi's family house.

It seemed everywhere we went there were plenty of steps and I fell down as I was going up to the second floor to our hotel room and bumped my lip and it was bleeding. Kofi hollered for ice for my lip that was swelling. I was grateful for the ice cube the waitress brought to me in her bare hands. This was one of many falls I had getting used to the new terrain but none so serious that I felt I needed x-rays.

The following day we had to get passport pictures and sign many forms. Chairman drove us home in our shiny new-to-us 'home used' brand new second hand red Toyota pick-up truck, while Fifi drove the other car.

Before we could get home it was dark and rainy, we were so glad someone else was driving because we couldn't see. The street lighting was poor, the roads were unfamiliar and other drivers were acting recklessly. Thanks to the Eternal Spirit for protecting us and allowing our mission to be accomplished. We arrived home safe and sound.

The next day Kofi was so happy to be driving where he wanted to go. Over and over he'd say can you believe it babe, I'm driving in Afrika! He loved his independence, now he could really take on Ghana! We named the truck Little Red Riding Hood because it was a bright red color.

Our friend Prof. Fifi soon after traveled with his wife and children to England to live and further his education. He did come home once and looked us up but we were not at home at the time. Our neighbors told us that he came to look for us. Ghanaians say "he met our absence." We would sure like to see him again.

A couple of months later Ann called us to say some folks from the village of Odonase where we donated items wanted to visit and thank us for our charity. We thought the gesture kind and set a date for their visit. Upon their arrival the two men and lady had a live goat on a leash and baskets of yam, cassava, plantain and oranges which they presented to us with appreciation for the good deed we did for their village school.

We accepted with joy but didn't know where to put the goat and there were many laughs over the matter. So we tied it up for the night on our veranda and the next day it was slaughtered for preparation of some good ole light soup. I am a city girl and had never even seen a chicken killed until coming here, and this is the first time I've eaten fresh killed anything. Also the fresh red snapper, sole fish and seafood we get here is so delicious from right out of the ocean.

Our new Abanyie family had prime property available on the main street called Kotokuraba Road. Ann showed it to us and I could hear Kofi's brain turning. I had no intention of working and was in retirement mode and I had no ideas to use the properties for. A week later Kofi told me he purchased some Afrikan artifacts from a guy who was closing his shop near Cape Coast Castle.

The seller brought the items to the house and they were beautiful. There were tall giraffes, drums, elephants, masks of all shapes and sizes, some bronzed and some were beaded and included oil paintings, jewelry, and small souvenir items. I asked the prices they should sell for and started cataloging for Kofi.

Kofi my love was a go getter and had to be doing something productive at all times. He saw what he thought was a good investment of four million Ghana Cedis and went for it. I had to admire him on one hand but who was going to run this boutique he wanted to open? He had decided to use one of the family stores as a barber shop and the one next door as a boutique. I couldn't muster up any enthusiasm. All I could do was watch Kofi go about his task full force.

Our landlord had a group of masons and carpenters which Kofi employed to start getting the stores ready. He designed cabinets and had them made. He bought tiles for the floors and paint for the walls. We traveled to Accra for barber chairs which turned out only to be office chairs they use as an alternative. He bought electrical supplies, plumbing parts, canopies and sign boards. He shopped for clothes to sell and sent for barber supplies from America and London.

My man is something to watch when he's on a mission. You either join in and help or get out of his way because he moves fast and runs circles around you. He can do everything that a laborer can do and has plenty of experience from his younger days on construction sites. He could be the foreman or contractor on any job he sets his mind to do.

Needless to say the list of unfinished work for the landlord was never completed in the house we rented. We got tired of asking him to complete the list of items with him not responding. We went on to complete the work because we take care of property as good stewards whether we own or lease it. We assumed the landlord would give us credit for doing the work that he should have done. Hence you know what assuming does, so you already know there was not a good outcome to this situation. As time went on Kofi even repainted the outside of the house. He didn't expect any compensation for this. He just wanted the house we lived in to be brightly painted. He liked things decent and orderly. We would later find out the landlord was not an appreciative man.

Most days I stayed at home finding things to do around the house but by the end of the week Kofi wanted me to come and see the progress being made in town at the stores. Things were really coming together and I realized he's a visionary who can look beyond appearances and see the potential in things and manifest them.

As Kofi plowed away at the tasks at hand the day quickly approached when the grand opening came. The shelves were filled with artifacts, the walls were decked with pictures and masks, the desks and office chairs in place, the barber stations were waiting their customers and Kofi decorated so creatively. All the items were priced tagged, inventory lists, business cards, and flyers were printed.

We placed a table, umbrella and chairs outside in front of the shops and followed the advice of our neighbor Mama T to place a shelf out front to place artifacts on it. When people passed they could see some of the items being sold inside the boutique. The barbershop doors were always opened and you could see it was sparkling clean with four stations. Kofi tore down a wall and made a passage way in the back of both stores so we could pass between the two and he made a bathroom. A toilet was something that probably no other store had. It was a year or two later that

Parliament made it mandatory that all building plans must include inside toilets for all homes, apartments and businesses.

As in the movie Field of Dreams, "if you build it they will come." Plenty people came for jobs and plenty people came to sell their wares, but customers were few. Kofi's experience as a licensed barber teacher, barber shop owner and manager in America prompted him to want to teach Ghanaians who were interested the proper use of barbering tools. He wasn't charging to teach but the student would have to buy their tools on a lay-away basis which Ghanaians call *lay—buy.*

The normal way to cut hair we'd seen while in Ghana was to use a razor blade while sitting on a stool under a tree. Young men walk around town carrying a sign with haircut styles on it and if you want a haircut you stop him and find a place to sit down and get your hair cut with a razor blade and a comb. They may even reuse the blade from person to person. Kofi wanted to raise awareness that barbers lack of proper hygiene techniques could lead to the spread of HIV-AIDS. He wanted to teach proper sanitation, sterilization of tools, some physiology, how to use anti-bacterial aides to prevent infection.

There were many barber kiosks which could fit one chair for the customer being served and one chair for a waiting customer. I have to admit Kofi's shop had taken the quality of Cape Coast barber shops up to a higher level. We had a few curious people and even one female but they never completed the application process. There were plenty barbers to come and go but they never bought tools for themselves, except for one young man named Kwamena. Over the year he worked Kofi deducted a small amount of money from his pay to pay for his tools.

Our shop was one of a kind in the area and people came from Takoradi and Kumasi to see it and buy some of the supplies for sale. The price of a haircut was less than $2.00 at 3,500.00 Ghana Cedis. When Kofi was present in the shop he made money but when he was not present he didn't make any money. He was told there were no customers.

While employing people Kofi learned to allow them to come and go freely. It was bad business to have people doing work they really didn't want to do and their attitude showed that they were only doing it for the money. Also he didn't expect people to stay in his employment forever because they should set goals to move ahead. It was hard getting used to people leaving without giving any notice, never sharing that they intended to leave. Some would collect their pay and never show up again.

Folks that behaved this way, leaving without giving the two week's notice Kofi requested, made us happy that they were gone, and it was okay if we never saw them again. When the parting was done in a respectful, timely manner with both parties amicable to the decision; we would be sorry to see them go but be willing to be of assistance to them if needed. If they came by to greet us at a later date we'd be happy to see them. Proprietors all say revolving doors are needed for the many people coming and going from the worksites for trivial reasons.

As for the boutique, a lot of visitors would come and go but mostly people who only wanted us to buy their wares to sell in the shop. Kofi had it set up so beautifully it was really a joy to be there. He would soon hire someone to manage the shops on a full time basis. Our place became a meeting spot where people could sit out front and have a cool drink and continue on their journey even if they didn't patronize the barber shop or the boutique. It was a good way to meet people. Kofi even joined the local business association and he opened an account for me in a local women's credit union.

Kotokuraba Road is the main street in Cape Coast and nothing goes on in town without coming down this street. All high officials pass here, the annual festival begins on this road, brass bands and parades all pass this mercantile area. Ann's relatives had foresight to buy property in this prime location and leave it for their children's children.

Kofi and I took Cape Coast by storm. We became popular fast and Kofi made his mark in the town. Folks were friendly and called out and waved to us as we drove around town. So many people knew of us but we had a lot to learn about our new locale and Cape Coasters.

"I am not ashamed of my grandparents
For having been slaves. I am only ashamed of myself
For having at one time being ashamed"
Ralph Ellison

18

Where Else Can An Afrikan Call Home?

We faced challenges however and nothing is 100 percent bed of roses. When our three-month stay was about up, we had to decide how to conduct ourselves. Although we felt we were home and wouldn't return to America, to the Ghanaian government we were only foreigners. We were emotionalizing our situation and some Ghanaians would tell us "don't mind them;-no one will ever put you out of Ghana." Of course we wanted to be law abiding and there were immigration laws to be followed. So our friend Ekow took us to the immigration department in Takoradi to apply for a visa extension to stay in the country.

Ghana only gives a two or three month visitors pass to stay in the country and then you must go to immigration for an extension. We were told that most of the time the renewal is only granted for an additional three months but, praises, we obtained a six month stay.

Truthfully, we never even thought of needing permission to stay in the country. We actually felt because we wanted to call Ghana home, that's all was required. Romanticism as it highest! The immigration officer said we had only come to Ghana to help ourselves; this was far from our truth so we didn't argue with him and thanked the Lord for the time granted.

We became perturbed about having to jump through hoops for the immigration dept. it was just too emotional of a subject for me. Founder President Kwame Nkrumah invited Afrikans from the Diaspora to come help Ghana develop. He said this while attending Lincoln University in our home state of Pennsylvania. Former President Jerry J. Rawlings is also known to have invited Afrikan Americans to come to Ghana and assist with the country's growth.

The whole world knows Afrikan Americans are from the continent of Afrika. Where else can an Afrikan call home? Yes, Marcus Garvey was right "Afrika for Afrikans, at home and abroad!" I plead with authorities to allow dual citizenship for those of us who want to make Ghana our home. Don't we have the right to return home?

Believe me, there is only a remnant of those wanting to come back; Afrika will not be flooded with people who want to repatriate here from outside. I don't want to give up my American citizenship because I still have family I love there and will visit them from time to time.

Some of us have to return overseas to work intermittently to increase finances in order to return and invest soundly in Ghana. All I see is a win-win situation for Ghana and those Diasporas who choose to make Ghana or any other Afrikan country their permanent home.

As long as we are law abiding, contributing economically and constructively to Afrika's growth, let our souls come and be at rest without the agitation of validating our passports monthly, quarterly, or yearly; it is a source of *wahala* for us (meaning trouble and suffering). I wish that immigration officers would put themselves in our shoes and try to understand our trauma regarding being separated from our homeland.

Every time we'd go to the immigration office in Cape Coast we'd get into an altercation with the officer handling our paperwork. Most often we're met with antagonism. We wrote African American as our nationality and every time they would cross out the word African arguing that our passports state we are Americans. Who wants to keep going through that nonsense repeatedly?

As for me it never lets me rest emotionally, spiritually, or physically, like an open sore never healing, digging up the subject of the Trans Atlantic Slave trade again and again; the reason why we were not born on the continent of Afrika in the first place.

Whoever is responsible to sanction dual citizenship for us who are the offspring of our ancestors who were shipped off the Afrikan continent during the Middle Passage; pass the law affirmatively because it is an idea whose time has come. Do the right thing. Give our Ancestors and their offspring some peace at last. Let us be 'free at last' just as Martin Luther King Jr. proclaimed.

"Please do not lose your temper here,
We are too busy to help you find it."
(Xerox copy slogan on the wall at a government office)

19

"A Bad Day In Ghana Is Better

Than A Good Day In The Usa"(Unknown)

Meanwhile at the barber shop and boutique we were learning how Cape Coast municipal and the Ghana Electricity Company conducted business. The electric bill hadn't been paid and the electricity utility truck pulled up and five or six guys jumped out and announced "we've come to shut off your service." We planned on paying at the beginning of the next month when the pension money came, however they said that would be too late.

The previous months' bill overlapped with the current month. They wouldn't allow us to go to the office to pay it right then, nor would they accept the money themselves, so they shut it off. Now we had to pay the bill plus a reconnection fee.

A friend we met at the electricity company later said unofficially if we had offered a small amount of money for them all to share; our lights would not have been shut off. He said he'd heard that we didn't even try hard not to have the service terminated. Meaning we hadn't offered any money as an incentive not to turn off the electricity. This same friend asked us for a loan of which he never repaid.

Can you believe while we were at the Cape Coast municipal office paying our business license fees the municipal workers task force was out on the street pad locking our doors at that same time! We just didn't seem to be flowing in the rhythm of the way things were done.

Welcome to Cape Coast Business District. Ghanaians pay for their television services via a T.V. license paid annually. I guess we weren't paying attention or didn't take it seriously enough. Kofi and I had laughed about what in the world is a T.V. license? So announcements were made to pay your fees for a time and by the time the task force comes; it's to punish those persons who haven't paid.

The task force was out on a Sunday morning with a usual gang of people; the guys were very belligerent and angry at us for flouting their laws and wrote up a citation to go to court the next day with a fine. When we went to the stores the next day and talked to our neighbor about it she asked her husband to help us; and he did.

Somehow he was able to have our file pulled and kept us from going to court. He felt insulted when we wanted to dash (tip) him for helping us. We were so thankful to him for keeping us out of the lions' den. We learned our lesson and promptly paid our T.V. license from then on.

All I can say is some of these folks seem to enjoy having the power to threaten and try to intimidate, they burst in on you with Gestapo tactics. The moral of these stories is to keep abreast of deadlines and make payments in a timely manner so not to face the task forces and their macho scare tactics. By the time they come out in full force they feel persons have scoffed at the law and they treat you accordingly. Some seem to get extreme pleasure to chastise folks that come from outside. We would do our best to avoid falling into these traps again in the future.

Still as it's said here, "a bad day in Ghana is better than a good day in USA." Ghana just feels good to my soul. Geographically, Ghana is located at the center of the world. I feel very balanced here in so many ways. It's hard to try to explain. It's like the adage the best things in life are free and how life is full of simple pleasures.

Our spiritual connection with mother earth: the cool breeze, the hot sun, the ocean, the beauty of the black skin, the red clay, black dirt, the white sand, the bright smiles, the sunset, the sunrise, the dignity of the people, the rhythms, nature, freedom, and it just feels good to me.

Like hearing Coltrane in the background, Billy Holiday singing lead, sipping a cold glass of bubbly, reading my favorite novel, smelling my favorite fragrance, hugging, kissing the one I love, sitting in my favorite spot, seeing children play, eating a nice piece of chocolate, laughing with friends, inhaling and exhaling, knowing the Creator's love and all the things that make me happy all rolled into one Ah . . . Ghana feels good to me. My whole being is satisfied as my feet stand on Afrikas' soil. I am so thankful, Lord.

I can say that the stresses here are experienced in a different dimension than the stressors in America. Here you can laugh stress away because some of the things that happen are so ludicrous. On the other side things seem so weighty and serious.

The battles that count aren't the ones for gold medals.
The struggles within yourself-the invisible inevitable battles
Inside all of us-that's where it's at.
Jesse Owens

Buying Land In Ghana, Class 101

Since we had permanent people to work in the shops Kofi and I started looking for land to buy to build something for ourselves. There was no need to delay perhaps by the time we'd leave our leased house we could be ready to move into our own space. Well it wasn't easy at all we found out and there was no systematic way to go about it. You have to scout around to find a piece of land you like and then try to find the right person to talk to about buying it. We looked in Cape Coast areas of Green Hill, Siwdo and we also explored Moree, Ampenyi, and Elmina.

When you find land you like, you must go "knocking" to the chief of the village where the land is if it is Stool land. Stool land is in custody of the chief and must have his and the community's approval to sell. The money from the sale must be shared among the people or for community use. If the land is family owned land then you must find the family head called the Ebusuapanyin. There will be a male and female head and all the family has to agree to the sale of the land.

Sometimes the wrong person will sell you land and that makes the sale invalid. I know people who have paid for their land twice over. I know folks who have built and then were taken to court and lost the case and lost all their money and property. There is no sure way around this. It's almost the luck of the draw you pray and hope for the best. We have some stories to tell.

We put the word out that we were looking for land. Ann had her driver once take us to Brenu Akynimu, Elmina for dinner and it was a fine coastal town. We talked with a man from the town named Ebow and asked him to lead us to the proper people to sell some land to us. We had to give him money to go around and find the appropriate persons to meet with us. This led to several palavers at our house where certain people who were for us getting the land would come –at-dinner-time to talk about how we had to have a lobby group of people in our favor to buy land before we approached the chief.

We finally met with the chief, his linguist (his speaker), because you don't speak directly to the chief, the chief's secretary, treasurer, youth leader and other witnesses were all present. Custom mandates that when you go "knocking" at the chief's door you send Schnapps, a liquor and if you don't have it you render the amount of money comparable to him. Of course we're told that local Schnapps wouldn't go over as well as an imported bottle which was more expensive. You also dash him an amount of money for his time. During this time the average amount was 25.00 Ghana Cedis.

We made our petition known to the chief's linguist who made our request known to the chief. He seemed as if the others were forcing him to do something he didn't want to do. As if he was being coerced but he said yes we could have some land.

The fun started. Nana (chief) asked us in private for a house and a car for himself. We had to honestly tell him we didn't have money like that. If we did that for him we wouldn't have money to build our own house. He never brought it up again I guess it was just worth a try to him.

We were taken to Brenu Beach and shown sixteen plots of land measuring 100 feet by 100 feet each right on the beach. Of course I knew this was my dream come true place to build our house. We took pictures and were so excited at the prospect of this land being ours.

Two of the town's people visited us with the town planning map for the area. It showed the proposed future development plan for the town. If we purchased the land we had to build a guesthouse on it. We hadn't planned on going into the hotel business but would do it to get that beautiful piece of land. Sixteen plots is four acres and almost too much for me to walk around but we would manage it.

We solicited the surveyor to measure, demarcate the land and draw up the site plan. At this time land was sold at a low price and they wanted approximately $270.00 in cedis for each plot of land. The total cost of the land would be the cedi equivalent of $4,320.00 and believe it or not our finances were dwindling down. We bargained to pay a deposit and the balance over a few months.

We heard there were factions in town between those who want the land sold to us and those who don't. We didn't understand what it was all about so we kept going after the land we wanted. We had to pay the surveyor to do his work and then we would go to the lands department to research if the land was owned by anyone.

Sister Ann escorted us to the municipal lands department and the clerk researched the information on the site plan to see if there was any record of someone having previous ownership of the land we wanted to purchase. We were told there was nothing noted about the piece of land we desired. We were then free to have an indenture (deed) drawn up and proceed to get it signed by the chief and witnesses.

At the same time we found that we were in the middle of a dispute that had nothing to do with us. We were still trying to find out the details. We sought the help of a lawyer from the town but lived in Takoradi and we rode back and forth to his home in hope of meeting with him several times and waited hours outside his home. The two people guiding us had us visit an elders home to seek his approval and he in his fragile state rode with us to persuade the lawyer that we be given the land. This man, Uncle C. said that the ancestors must have led us to their town and we could even be long lost relatives. He was not strong physically and we purchased some medicine for him that he needed.

We finally had our encounter with the lawyer and he assured us that the property was unencumbered and we could go ahead with the purchase. He said that promises to develop the land had not been kept in over ten years; and now since we as the new buyers were interested, the land could be sold and he'd have the papers drawn up. When the necessary documents were drawn up we paid our deposit.

Our brother Ricky was present as a witness for us and the deed had to be taken to court and stamped. All of this took place the months of April/May the year 2000. Our deed was dated 14th May 2000.

We didn't want to focus on all the confusion that was going on about us concerning the land. Promise Land always has to be taken by force spiritually. This land was too beautiful to be relinquished so easily; after all we now had our papers. We went ahead to have our architectural drawings of the house/hotel completed and sent to the district town planning office for approval.

In the meantime Kofi went ahead and bought wood boards, sand, stones, cement, tarp, shovels, and hammers, work boots etc. and had them delivered to the site. He built a tool shed to put supplies in and it doubled as a place where a watchman could stay at night. Kofi had the land cleared and was ready to begin making a profile of the house and start digging the foundation. He hired masons, carpenters, laborers and bought hard hats for them, making it a real construction site.

Sadly the elder Uncle C. who traveled with us became hospitalized and we visited him but he passed away soon after. The town people had so many theories on why he died. Although he was over eighty years old, it seemed you can't just die a natural death here. Some said he had bullets and arrows in his body "spiritually" and that he was killed because he sided with us. All kinds of myths and mind manipulations about juju were described. We attended his funeral and gave a substantial donation. He bonded to Kofi and me right away and we appreciated him being an ally of ours. May he rest in perfect peace!

During this time of going up and down and round and around I was getting dispirited and remember writing to my son telling him if anything happen to us he should check on certain people that I gave him the names of. I don't know why purchasing plots of land had to have such a frenzied process. I know I was probably physically and emotionally weary of the lack of a systematic way of doing things. Little did we know that the worst was yet to come!

The lawyer kept maintaining the land was for us, and people would tell us "don't mind them." So Kofi kept plugging away, going to the site daily, giving work orders and putting his vision into action. On a certain day when Kofi and the workers attempted to drive through the beach gate to get to our property he was stopped by guards. As he got out of the truck to ask the men what was the problem, one of them pushed him and told him he was trespassing. Kofi didn't insist to go through the gate but found a foot path to walk the supplies he brought; it was about a mile walk and he and his employees finished the work day still.

Ann suggested we go to the head of our municipal district for help. She went with us to see the district chief, and after we told him our problems and asked for his assistance he calmly said to us "I will never sign your building plan, I was waiting for you to build your hotel so I could come and bulldoze it down." I immediately got up to leave since it was obvious there was no help to be found at this government office. So now the prospects were not looking good at all concerning our "Promised Land." This was what Kofi wanted to name our place.

Then another beautiful day in Ghana there was a knock on our door by a policeman. He asked for Kofi who was not in at the time, and he told me we were invited to the police station to speak to the captain. He didn't say why we should come, just show up. I called my sister Ann immediately to report what happened and she said she'd accompany us there.

Kofi wasn't disturbed when I told him we were invited to go to the police station. He just smiled and said do I have to accept the invitation? Ann told us yes we'd better go as soon as possible and she'll meet us there. We proceeded to Cape Coast Central Police Station, met Ann and were led to the captain's office. He greeted us, then banged on his desk and hollered "how did you come by that land?" "You cannot have that land!" He said Kofi and I were a threat to the peace and the security of the area. Imagine that!

We inquired why weren't the people who sold us the land also invited to his office. We've come to Ghana and were led around by some Ghanaians and as far as we knew we had not committed any crime.

So we were told officially that we could not build on the proposed site; if we were to continue going there daily pursuing our dream we would be breaking the law. Dreams seem to die and all appears to be lost but don't lose all of your hope, let a mustard seed of faith rise from the ashes. If this was not the property then there must be another. Our God is able!

Lastly, we were summoned to another government office whose director wanted to show us the power of attorney papers he held for the beach property that was sold to us. It did say the property was in their possession for the past thirteen years. This was when we found out that the villagers used the cash deposit we gave them to take this agency to court in attempts to take back control of their property.

They took this action because no development had come to the town since this agency managed the property. The town's people legitimately felt they could go to court to retrieve their property and give it to other potential buyers, namely the two of us and other Afrikan Americans. This only put us smack dab in the middle of a dispute that started long before we arrived in the country and put us in a no win situation.

Of course we tried appealing to all quarters to reconsider or provide another beachfront land for our cash deposit. We tallied up the monies spent in total during our efforts to acquire the property from beginning to end. We wrote to the lawyer several times, we wrote to the chief of the town, the land committee, and to the government agency head. No one bothered to answer us except the lawyer. We asked him for the money back that we paid him but he said no-his services were rendered by drawing up the deed paperwork. Never mind that the paperwork was worthless to us.

We took an accounting of what we spent since the start of this fiasco: first having the four acres cleared, purchase of cutlasses and hammers, saws, helmets, flashlights, that by the way were never returned to us. We hired security guards, carpenters, masons, laborers, bought documents, surveys, building plans, site plans, lawyer fees, knocking fees, dashes upon dashes, petrol (gasoline), drink money, chop money (food), transport, sand, stones, cement, wood, tarps, nails, rope, boots, pillars (bought twice because someone broke the first ones we put up) and our cash deposit. The estimated total came to approximately 14 million cedis which meant we had wasted over $3000.00 and had nothing to show for it.

Notwithstanding the inner turmoil of being shamed, mistreated, disrespected, invited to the police station and talked to as if we were criminals, and my Kofi was physically assaulted by a guard and told he was trespassing. This guard was a neighbor who later apologized to Kofi before he died. Broken dreams and many tears but yet we still had a glimmer of hope that our Creator still had something good in store for us. We were down but not out. This was our first lesson on buying land in Ghana, class 101.

I do have to disclose that the problems buying land are not exclusive to foreigners. Ghanaians also have their share of land disputes. The courts are full of cases regarding land title issues.

"Without a struggle there can be no progress"
Fredrick Douglas

21

If At First You Don't Succeed, Try Again

Kofi didn't waste time going after another property. Sister Ann told us of a plot she owned in Cape Coast and as soon as Kofi had someone weed and clear the land a woman approached him and said he was on her property. This made Ann and the woman have to go to court to see who had the true indenture. Ann's indenture was older than the litigants we later found out but we decided to abort that property.

We tried the State Housing Corporation in Cape Coast. The representative would show us places that we were not fond of. Still looking for ocean view land our brother and sister took us to meet the chief of another village. He assured us there was land in his town we could acquire but the land was adjacent to a shrine and the owner in the house behind it had strange designs and writing outside his house which looked like something out of a Stephen King movie.

Kofi didn't like the way the property was situated and felt it was at a dead end. This didn't sit well with him as a former military man. There was also a school building blocking the view and to this the chief said it would soon be demolished because a new school had been built. I wanted to be at the ocean so badly that I was willing to still purchase this piece of land.

Kofi was willing to try for it only because I wanted it despite his misgivings.

However every time the chief would send a message for us to meet him at his palace, when we arrived to see him he would not be there. This happened several times so we assumed he was not serious. There was brother Kojo Bey who had purchased land from this same chief two years prior to our coming and he never acquired his land due to dispute. A couple of years later we heard this same chief had his "sandals taken away" meaning he was taken from the throne by his town people and chased out of town for his wayward behavior.

We looked at other sites in Elmina but really didn't like the areas because they weren't near the ocean. So we tried in Moree which was up on a hill facing the ocean and the chief was willing to sell it to us. Unfortunately we would need to spend too much money to make an access road to the plots of land. One architectural company representative visited the site with us and was to wait for us to give him the go ahead to do an actuarial study to show how much it would cost to prepare the land for us to build on. However he didn't wait and prepared the paperwork and brought it to us for his fee. His fee was exorbitant and the cost to get the land prepared to build on was too costly. We didn't pay him because he jumped the gun and did the report before we authorized him to, we also decided against buying that property.

Green Hill was a lovely place with an ocean view and there was a house already built selling for fifty thousand dollars outright, no mortgage, by then that was out of our range. The two businesses were not thriving at all and never covered the salaries or the utilities. Our bank account was dwindling and we'd soon be depending on our monthly pensions just to live. The picturesque view of the ocean, green valleys and nearby village made me want to fall on my knees in worship to our Creator. Whoever buys that home has a million dollar view!

We tried another real estate agent who showed us beach front land in yet another town but the price was $5000.00 for one plot. Things appeared to be going from bad to worse, rising prices, knocking fees, going in circles and still coming up empty. I cried out to God, where's the land you have with our name on it?

I was getting worn out from looking for land but Kofi was still inquiring. He came home one day and said he bought some land and wanted me to see it. I replied to him I'll just wait awhile and see if you're able to keep it. He said he had asked the owners of a filling (gas) station at the junction of Brenu Road if he could set up some of our arts and crafts on their corner to sell to people passing by to the beach.

The owner declined him but when the chief of the town heard he was looking for land he showed him land opposite that place and offered it to him for sale. Kofi said he liked it and felt that I would also so he agreed to buy it and he gave the chief a deposit.

I was so disappointed by the various unfruitful land deals that I didn't even go to see this property for at least a month; meanwhile Kofi hired laborers to clear the land and had built a tool shed before I'd even seen the site.

He begged me to come with him one weekend and take some arts and crafts to display that people going back and forth to the beach might stop to purchase.

Every weekend Kofi would display items from the boutique at our new site in the hopes of making some sales, but I don't remember even one sale. The cars drove by so fast to the beach they never slowed down to see what we sold. I loved this man, always trying and determined to risk failing rather than to do nothing at all.

He was one tenacious man who felt he had to find a place for us to settle down at all costs. I would fill over two dozen water bottles and freeze them for Kofi to take to the work site daily for his workers. Somehow I believed any day he would come home with the news that something went wrong with his land deal.

However I was satisfied with the location once visiting the site because it was on the Accra-Takoradi Road in the town of Ayensudo, Elmina at the turn for Brenu Beach. We were five kilometers from the land at the beach that we didn't get previously.

Kofi had hired twenty-three laborers to clear the land that was thick bush. He hired a young guy named Yaw to be his foreman, and Peter right out of Takoradi Polytechnic as his carpenter, some area masons, and he himself was the contractor.

The workers would stay on the property while Kofi commuted daily from Cape Coast to Elmina a thirty minute drive each way.

The land was sold to us by Chief Nana Afrakoh of Ayensudo in Elmina. He and his brother Cobbina were the custodians of this family land and they told us to go ahead and start building and assured us no one would ever come to give us any problem about this particular land.

They were right because even ten years later our guesthouse is built on this land and we've had no problems. Nana Afrakoh didn't have the money to have his land surveyed and he didn't trust to get all of his acreage by allowing government surveyors to do the job. He felt some acres would be lost to him in the process; but we never had any problem with this land site to this day.

Our indenture was for one and quarter acres of land. However there was a problem at the court saying that the government surveyors' handwriting on the indenture (deed) was forged and had to be redone.

We had to get a new indenture, obtain the chiefs' and witness's signatures, resign ourselves, and get a certified surveyor to sign and return it to the court for stamping. Some months later we completed this task.

Yes it seems I lost my faith a bit but thankfully, Kofi did not lose his. Over the years it would be like this, when one of us was disappointed and not feeling like putting up with madness of how some things are done here; always one of us had the energy to push ahead to do what was needed to press towards our future goals. As it was I couldn't let go of the beach land and was determined to get some ocean front land for the money that we'd already paid. I would get back on the case attempting to settle that as soon as we were settled into our own permanent space.

Success is to be measured not so much by the
Position that one has reached in life as much as
By the obstacles which he has overcome while
Trying to succeed
Booker T. Washington

Down And Out In Ghana

Meanwhile the lease was about to end at the house we were renting and we had Ann to ask the landlord if he'd consider granting us additional time for the extra money we put into beautifying his place and for completing some items that he should have fixed when we moved in. He quickly answered no to this request. I replied to him we didn't have to agree to move into his house and we could have done our research and might have found a place better than his and even cheaper. I was so angry with him for being ungrateful towards us. Well, at this comment our sister Ann became offended; although I was not directing my statement to her but to the landlord.

I remember so clearly another time we were with the family at Zion house on the same day the 9/11 tragedy in America Sept. 11, 2001 was on the news as the plane was going into the second tower. I inwardly wanted to fall on my knees in prayer for the people dying in the Twin Towers. Yet we found ourselves in a situation where our aunties were attempting to mediate between us and Ann. Kofi said "no one will be on our side and that they'd be on the landlords' side." Our dear sister walked out and stopped speaking to us for many months. So we left the family house without a resolve that day and didn't talk to them again for the next six months. All this was a misunderstanding.

Kofi became ill and the landlord was among some of the business association members to visit him in the hospital. As the visitors were leaving he lagged behind and had the nerve to ask me then and there in the hospital when would we be leaving his house?

I told him the end of the year and that would have put us two months overdue the lease. He told me "You will pay!" Kofi was discharged from the hospital and was not any better. Our friend Yacubu (Now of blessed memory) would visit and see how Kofi was literally lifeless, lying on the couch, barely eating and had no energy.

Our friend Yacubu visited and saw Kofi's poor condition and exclaimed he was going to bring a friend of his who worked in a lab clinic, who was so knowledgeable they call him a doctor. I can't sit here and watch my father die he said. The "Dr." arrived with mega vitamins which he gave by injection, some blood tonic and administered them to Kofi; fifth-teen minutes later Kofi said he was hungry and ate some food. The lab work showed that his hemoglobin level was below seven, like a child's.

Praise God from whom all blessings flow. Kofi was still weak but he was taking in nourishment and rebounding. However he was too weak and couldn't help me pack so I started packing up our belongings so we could soon move out of the landlord's house.

A week later I took Kofi to see the "doctor" and while there I saw a man with a truck large enough to move our things and I asked him if he could do that for us on the weekend. We only had two hundred thousand Ghana cedis (about twenty dollars) to our name and the man said he would accept it but we had to move the very same day. So he rode us home and I asked our neighbors to help me load the truck, swept the place clean and we left Aquarium Down, Cape Coast.

My sweetie by then built six hotel rooms but only one was completed enough to live in, and we moved right in. He had also built three storerooms so there was plenty of room to store our items. When the movers assembled the bed I let Kofi rest right away. Then I managed to direct the people helping me where to place our things. We lost a few items in the transition but hallelujah we were free in the place my husband provided for us. What a glorious feeling! We were now in our own chalet on our own land built by my baby. Thank you Jesus!

Our good friend Auntie Gladys was leaving for the States and there was a going away party for her at Fairhill Guesthouse in Cape Coast, our sister's place. I was not able to leave Kofi to attend so I sent something to be read to her in our behalf and also sent the keys to the house to Ann to give to the landlord. Ann sent them back to me with the massage we had to meet with the landlord and do a walk through the house and give the keys to the landlord ourselves on Monday morning.

These months that Kofi and I and our dear sister didn't talk to each other was the saddest point of our time since in Ghana. It was a misunderstanding; angry words said in reference to the landlord that sister had taken to heart. We would never do anything to hurt Ann who poured out her heart and soul for us since the beginning. Kofi and I were really hurt by the strained relationship and pride allowed us to let it go on too long. We felt why get angry at us for something we said to the landlord?

Also during this time our social security checks had been tied up because we applied to have them direct deposited back to our bank account in the USA. We wanted to stop traveling to Accra monthly to pick up our pension checks because the day trip was grueling. Often times the check would be delayed or rerouted to another part of the world and we wouldn't find out until we arrived at the embassy. The mistake we made was to change both of them at the same time. We should have only put the transfer in for one check at a time and then we'd have one to live on. So it took six months of calling Social Security Administration and visiting the American Embassy to finally get the paperwork straight.

The Embassy did allow us to borrow money of which we could repay when our finances were back on track. However it was in the fifth month without finances when the loan was approved. If you repay the loan in thirty days or less its interest free. God only knows how we managed those months without our monthly allotments.

By grace we were given credit by some Ghanaian merchants, one in particular was Pa Kwesie who patiently allowed us to shop in his store once a month and credit items. It appeared that we were lying because every month we'd say our money should come next month and it didn't come for five months until we borrowed from the Am. Embassy.

Some from our family of African Americans who knew our situation gave us money of which we returned when we were able. Alfred of Goil station allowed us credit for gasoline over those months and we appreciate all the kind Ghanaians who believed in us to repay the items they credited us. It is not easy to get credit in Ghana. Maybe folks could see that we were sincere and respected the things we were doing, I don't know. All I know "God's grace was sufficient for us." The Creator provided and we were grateful.

There were some folks who didn't take our plight well and worried us enough to repay the money for building supplies we credited and rightly so. Make a note to only change one social security check at a time if you're a couple so that at least you'll have one check to live on while waiting on SSA to process the paperwork. This was the hardest financial challenge we had here to date.

Kofi went around to barbershops and beauty shops selling his barber supplies cheap in order to gain some money. Reluctantly he even sold the jazz drums he purchased and enjoyed playing to relieve stress. Our dear friend Dr. Nana Malkia Brantuo "Big Mama" purchased them for Nana Kweku her grandson now of Blessed Memory.

We really needed the money but I was sad to see those drums go that gave Kofi so much pleasure to play. He'd come in from the day's work on the site and play some Coltrane or Miles Davis, put on his headphones and work on those drums. I don't know how the neighbors liked it though they never complained to us, but I knew it was good therapy for him.

The funniest story about those drums is how Kofi kept saying he wanted drums but I had to finally force him to travel to Accra to purchase them. He found a set that he liked, bought them and we took them back to the hotel room we were staying for the weekend.

We went to the Golden Tulip that evening for dinner to hear a jazz trio with singer Jimmy Beckley. Kofi was into the music so strong something possessed him to jump on stage and he tried to take the drummers sticks out of the drummer's hands. He seriously wanted to play some drums. The drummer refused to allow Kofi to take the drumsticks from him so Kofi displaced a bongo drummer from his drum and proceeded to bang away with the band. They let him play to his hearts' content and the audience cheered him on too. Go Baby! Yes I gave the drummer some!

"I have a bias against war, a bias for peace. I have a bias
Which leads me to believe that no problem of
Human Relations is ever insoluble."
Ralph Bunche

Three Little Words-Please Forgive Us

There was a meeting at Mable's Table Restaurant where the American
Embassy ambassador was visiting to speak in the Central region. This
was the first time we saw our Ghanaian family again in about six months.
Ann, Ricky, and big sister Aggie was in attendance and we all greeted each
other but the atmosphere was still cool between us.

A few weeks later I bought a card asking for forgiveness, saying we
were sorry and please forgive us. The Bible says if someone has something
against you, then you go to them and try to settle it. Auntie Leticia begged
Ann to patch up our relationship and she consented. It took some time
but I can truly say all is well between us at last. We are all back in love
again. One big happy family ever since.

We now say "what God has joined together, let no one put asunder."

Family may have disagreements but they remain family. There will
be conflicts but as long as you make up, that's what makes relationships,
friends and family. We may have left our biological family in America
and we miss them dearly and yet the family that God has given us here in
Ghana is just as precious to us.

Words cannot express the depth of feelings resulting from longing
and wondering where is the Afrikan family we were torn from? Who were

my ancestors? Kofi and I could only trace our family roots back to our maternal grandmothers and no further. We never knew our grand-fathers nor could trace our lineage back to our great-grandparents. This was a source of sorrow for us and is the case for a large number of American Afrikans.

Where are my uncles and aunties, sisters and brothers from my Afrikan roots? I cannot even find the words to express the depth of pain I'd feel when I'd ponder these things, especially when we were in the states and since we were estranged from Ann.

Afrikan family ties were never respected, with families torn apart. Our women were violated and the males sent far way, women sent over yonder, children stolen away, brothers and sisters separated to serve in other folk's homes. The remembrance of it hurts so.

These are all valid reasons to support the proposal for advocating reparations. How can the loss of one's country, culture, language, and history ever be compensated for? The loss is so great with infinite amount of monies indebtedness.

Thankfully we connected to an entire family that embraced us heart and soul. We've been to the gravesites in the village Odonase in Cape Coast where the ancestors of the Abanyie family are buried. Our sister Aggie said come and see where your grandparents are laid and we shed tears of gratitude for being engrafted into this loving, devoted clan. We didn't lament again, we have come home and we found our Afrikan family. We've been accepted and we accept that we've found our Afrikan roots. We came full circle.

Our Aunt Elizabeth is homebound and we call each other on the phone from time to time and when I'm in her neighborhood I stop in to see her. So this time I called and she greeted me with "Oh Adjoa it's a long time since we've seen ourselves." I missed her too.

Kofi and I realized we had been so busy and distracted with settling in, attempting to plant our roots, time had gone by so fast and now that we were reunited with our Afrikan family-it was time for us to be married in the community of family and friends.

Kofi and I were married October 6, 2002 by our new friend Rabbi Nathaniel Halevi in a Hebrew tradition wedding with our Abanyie family and small gathering of friends present. We surprised everyone who thought they were coming for our birthday party. However those in attendance were witnesses to our wedding ceremony. We had on matching outfits and I had an old traditional African hairdo with tight bands around my head that held it in place with beautiful gold filled ornaments and ribbon on top called Oduku. It hurt like a vice and only lasted till evening when I had to take it off.

We were married at our unfinished hotel site under our summer hut, an open air area to sit, eat and drink. Kofi looked so handsome, I loved Kofi so much, he was my soul mate, and if we never had a ceremony nothing would ever change that. We could have just jumped over a broom. I meant my vows to be with him till death and that I would never leave him nor forsake him. Even though we had a difference of opinion the same morning, he'll always be the only man for me.

He cherished me and his actions were unmistakable and undeniable, I knew I was loved. It was a good feeling, he was a good provider and I was secure in our love. I could lay my head on his shoulders and put my troubles in his pocket because he had my back. Kofi was a principled man who loved God. He was a self-actualized person and was pleased with himself. We were very happy to be together in Ghana.

Our family always said we were two peas in a pod. He had a jealous streak although I gave him no reason to mistrust me. He was spry and more energetic than I could ever be and we were a good match. He was a master at everything he put his hands to do, and I do mean everything.

24

Home Sweet Home

Kofi worked hard building Esteem Kofi and Adjoa Enterprises Limited in Ayensudo, Elmina. He never asked me nor talked to me regarding my thoughts on running a hotel, but he was the first to find out that I was in retirement mode and he agreed to find someone to manage the site. He simply said we needed something to do and a way to provide some jobs, so the first thing he built was the summer hut restaurant, bar, and kitchen. We were planting our roots deep in this small quiet village as twenty-first century pioneers.

Kofi put up a bamboo fence because the people in the village would trespass through the property. They were used to walking a shortcut path to their farms via our property. Some people actually said to us that they were here first and now we were fencing in the area blocking them out. We told them all they had to do was walk around the fence and could no longer use our property as a thoroughfare.

Still as time went on there would be fires set outside our fences, first on the east side then the west side, sometimes as soon as we put one fire out another one would start at a different location. If this was a scare tactic to run us away it was not going to work. Some said it was result of bush fires that can start during the dry season as the sun could spark fire with dry leaves and brush. We didn't believe the latter was the case.

Once we called the fire department and they didn't have petrol; the next time there was no water and they didn't come. We were told that there was water in this town but it wasn't until after we purchased the land we found out that we lived in a crisis area where the water only would come through the tap once a week. Surrounding villages in the area all shared the water pipe one day out of the week.

We installed two overhead water storage tanks and we learned to buy plenty of buckets to fill with water and have our employees learn to act as a fire brigade, one person filling the water buckets and passing to the others to throw onto the fire. We also filled buckets with sand to stamp out fire. So we were prepared. The firemen trained us how to put out fires and explained the proper equipment to purchase and how to use extinguishers correctly.

Children in our area would walk a mile to fetch water and return to their homes before they went to school in the mornings. Most of the time they gathered water from a pond or creek that was muddy. In some areas even dirty water is precious. They are taught to filter the water and boil it before they drink, I pray that they do. We found ourselves transporting the water dept. workers around who turn on the water pipe so that we'd be sure to get the tap turned on in our own village.

Once one of the men didn't sit well on the back of our pick-up and fell off as Kofi made a turn. He banged himself up real good with scratches and bruises. Although some friends were waiting to go out to dinner with us, we were tied up in the emergency ward and then at the pharmacy. We made sure he was taken care of.

He called his family and they came to take him home. One month later the man shows up with his older brother to admonish us for not coming to check on him at home and demanded that we owed him money for being out of work. We hadn't visited him because we didn't know where he lived nor had taken his number.

We thought we acted responsibly by taking him to the hospital and paid for his care and medicine. However we apologized and gave him some cedis for being out of work for a month. We went through all this because he didn't sit well on the truck. Needless to say we infrequently gave lifts to people on the back of our pick-up truck after that experience.

We became tired of traveling around buying water from other people's wells. Sometimes the water would spill out before we reached home. One day I asked Kofi couldn't we dig our own well? One week later after hiring some laborers to dig down about nine feet, we touched water. The guys made cement blocks and laid them the length of the well and we were dropping our own buckets down our own well at last.

We could use this water for everything except drinking because it was salty due to our close proximity to the ocean. We were purchasing bottled water to drink and cook with. However years later the Ghana Water Company renovated many of the water pipe systems and now water is available at least in our town every time we turn on the tap. This is a blessing many villages here do not have.

Our friends Gerri and Arnold Polk are missionaries whose work is to go around to villages without piped water and show them how to build rain water catchment and treatment systems. Pastors Enoch and Lagretta Butler have an NGO which addresses the needs of their congregation in a holistic way feeding spirit, soul and body along with methods to utilize rain water. These are some of our friends who live in Greater Accra when they come to Ghana. There is plenty of rain to be harvested especially during the rainy seasons which come in March to July and again in September and October.

Living in the village of Ayensudo, Elmina we had to get used to our neighbor's chickens roaming on our side every day; also the roosters who perch outside our bedroom window like clockwork, every blessed morning 6a.m.; and all of the mother hens with all her chicks and chickens always crossing the road.

My neighbors are now raising (jive) turkeys which join the chickens to come and eat the grass on our side of the fence. They squeeze under the fence and we can't keep them out. A turkey was on the roof of our summer hut restaurant, boy did I want to get Kofi's shotgun and cap him.

Five to six a.m. all the birds begin to compete to see who can sing the loudest and sweetest songs. They really praise God for the new day!

Then there's the village goats who love to come chop on our palm trees several times a day. The lizards who like being observed doing pushups and a few scorpions after the rainy season. Kofi said they killed a snake almost daily when they first cleared the land and I'm glad I wasn't around for that.

One neighbor was raising cows and bulls. Some children had been taunting them and ran away when Kofi just happened to be walking near them at one end of our property. One angry bull cornered him against the fence and was acting as if he were going to charge head on into Kofi. The bull was nodding his head and pacing up and down. Kofi was talking softly and slowly, "whoa-whoa."

Onlookers called for the owners of the bull who came just in time I believe to save Kofi's life. My husband, a small framed man could have never sustained the large animal crashing into him. Kofi said he prayed fervently and felt just like Daniel in the lion's den. Needless to say the bulls and cows had to be relocated to another area. It was like living on Old McDonalds farm but we didn't even own the animals.

We accepted the "home owner" gecko as part of the ambiance of living here. It's said this small lizard looking animal lives in huts and palaces alike, just like spiders do. We once tried to raise goats we bought a pregnant female and a young male. We didn't know what we were doing and depended upon our help to tend to them. They developed some type of disease which the vet said came from eating some bad leaves and we had to get rid of them.

We tried to have dogs and they all wound up dead. Two were hit by a car; two died mysteriously and appeared poisoned. The two dogs hit by cars wound up in the soup pots of some of our workers. When we told the guys to bury the dogs they answered "no please." They wanted to take them home. If they could be a blessing to someone in their death, we had no problem. Just don't use our pots to cook it and no we didn't want to taste it. We gave up on having animals.

We have plenty of species of birds that sweetly wake us up in the morning and serenade us at evening time. Then there are the obnoxious crows, and if anyone knows something that repels them please let us know because they like to pick the straw out of our huts and eat the fruit off of our trees.

We had a good cat named Matilda who had many litters which we gave away. She was our exterminator for field mice and garden snakes. She'd soar through the air catching birds flying near, and caught several lizards too. She died and we have one of her grand cats with us now.

There are some animals that are not allowed in some villages. In Ayensudo it's said their gods don't like dogs (I think that is why ours all died.) and in Brenu, Elmina their gods don't want goats or dogs in their village but sheep are allowed. Living here with nature is like being in one large science class. The various foliages and host of beautiful flowers seems endless, all kinds of insects and butterflies. We get twelve hours of daylight and twelve hours of darkness which comes 6:30 pm. It's beautiful watching the sunrise come up as if it's sitting on top of the ocean before it ascends.

Let there be light and there was light!
Gen. 1:3 KJV

Let There Be Light

Upon our arrival we were introduced to the electricity service going on and off. This would happen sometimes several times in the day like five or six times, or just the electricity remaining off for several hours during the day or night. As the years passed by we noticed every time it rains in our area the lights go off.

There was a time when the Akosomobo Dam where the water is stored that provides the energy for the country's electrical system was very low and we had what was termed 'load shedding' which meant we'd share the electrical service across the country.

Sometimes we'd have two days service on and one day without service. You should hear the shouts of joy in the village when the lights go out and come back on rather quickly; especially when there's a soccer game on. This is one of the things that are not normal but you learn to accept as normal and say thank you Lord when the light resumes. At least when we lived in Aquarium Down in Cape Coast we had electricity.

However when we purchased our land in Ayensudo, Elmina there was no electricity in the area. We were really pioneering and we adjusted well. It was rather romantic for us except for the lack of refrigeration. We had to travel daily to Elmina Market to buy ice blocks to keep our perishables and have cold drinks. I was with my man and he was with me so we just enjoyed our journey; accepting Ghana as it was.

We felt that life was simpler here and different, we found we could live on less, not needing all the frills we depended on in America. The change felt good. We were *living off the grid* before it became popular in the United States. We were looking at life from a different perspective, using a different side of our brain. Most things here are opposite of what we were used to, not right or wrong but unique.

Kofi bought a black and white television set and hooked it up to the truck at night so we'd have some sort of entertainment besides radio. Folks came around from the village to watch with us and plenty children, before long there'd be a large crowd enjoying.

Our village had been scheduled for the low-income electricity program for years before we moved there. The villager's were to come up with the money for a certain amount of electric poles and the government would subsidize the remainder of the project. It had just been a long time coming.

People told us things only get done in a presidential campaign year when candidates want to obtain votes. We'd been using candles, gas lamps, and torches (flashlights). We used a generator which cost about 150 Ghana Cedis a month for petrol. On nights when the full moon was out very bright, sitting under the stars at night was a virtual planetarium and so beautiful.

Two and a half years later Kofi saw a popular MP (Member of Parliament) at the ministries in Cape Coast. The minister was about to get in his chauffeured-armed guarded vehicle when Kofi approached him saying "Sir, you've got to help us, please help us." The guard was about to handle Kofi when the minister told the officer to stand down. He listened to Kofi tell our story of how we needed to have electricity because we wanted to open our guesthouse. The honorable minister told us to write him a letter and deliver it to his office, and we did as he said. He assured us he would look into the matter.

A few months later the minister was made to govern over the department of energy, and true to his word he visited our village. Our chief, nananom from surrounding areas, and various citizens were present to hear him speak at our facility. He talked to the people in their native tongue but we could understand he did say he would see to it that electricity would come to our town due to my Kofi pleading with him on the street.

Kofi and I decided to remain apart from Ghana's politics in the public eye. We came in on the tail end of President Rawlings tenure and we saw the peaceful changing over of power to the Kufuor government. We didn't identify with any political party and not interested in voting if we could. We didn't know the history enough to be savvy in discussing Ghana's politic. Of course we had our own private opinions but in public "no comment please." We hoped to have the sympathetic ear of whoever was in power to address needs and issues pertinent to our particular predicament as returnees from the Diaspora.

The next presidential campaign year the same honorable minister decided to campaign for President of Ghana, during this time he visited our community and the folks gathered at our place again. He told them that our village never voted for him but electricity will come because of my husbands' appeal to him; and that any investors who comes to Ghana and has built as we have should have all the facilities they need to do business.

I won't go into all the horror stories and details of laborers carrying those heavy poles to our place and we not having money at the time to dash them for carrying them. They carried those heavy poles away and said when the "money comes" they'd bring the poles back again. Nor will I go into how when they tried to dig the ground to install the electric poles there were so many big boulders in our compound that we had to hire a bulldozer to dig them out. Still we give thanks!

So this is how electricity came to the village of Ayensudo, Elmina and when the honorable minister came to our village the third time it was to officially launch the start of the power service and turn on the lights. He asked of Esteem Kofi but we were given a different time for the program and weren't present. How do you like that? On a very sad note while the lights came on the first night, one little girl became so excited and didn't watch well crossing the highway. She was hit by a car and it was fatal. This was so sad for our community. May her soul rest well, Amen

Black people have always been America's
Wilderness in search of a promised land
Cornel West

Alien Resident In The Land Of My Ancestral Roots

In so far as the businesses were not profitable and we moved to Elmina
district thirty minutes outside of Cape Coast, we thought it better to turn
the properties (barber shop and boutique) back over to the family. Sister
Aggie escorted us to the Ghana Investment Promotion Center where we
found out we should not have been in the retail sales business as alien
residents. (I hate that term.)

The hotel business was an appropriate enterprise as foreign investors
and Kofi had already started building a hotel so we were able to transfer
businesses. I think it is appropriate here to note that Kofi had to have been
led by Spirit to move rightly into the hotel business. Spirit knew what was
coming around the corner that we could not see.

We had to change all our paperwork to reflect the changes in the
businesses and all this costs money of course. Yet the question we all should
be asking is how did they allow us to go into the barbering business and
wood craft boutique in the first place? I'll try to make a long story short.

While we were having our immigration challenges a friend had a
friend earlier take us to Ghana Investment Promotion Center (GIPC)
to learn how to be able to stay in the country as investors. We were told
if we invested $50,000.00 or more we could be the sole owners of a
corporation or a sole proprietorship. The other option was to take on

a Ghanaian partner and $10,000.00 would be the required investment money. However Kofi and I had already invested over fifty thousand dollars between the two shops we had, the house we leased for two and half years and the hotel we were still building. We only had to go back and recoup all the receipts and amounts of money we brought in since our arrival to the country. Kofi didn't want to have anyone else partner with us, so to be the sole owner of the corporation. Kofi was named as the Managing Director and I as assistant and the gentleman who escorted us was named as our secretary. Somehow it was assumed by GIPC personnel that the man escorting us was our ten percent partner and he was included when the paperwork was written up.

Retail sales, barbering, beautician, and taxi driving are the only restricted occupations for foreigners; so we never should have been allowed to go into the previous vocations. The initial paperwork and then to change over from one profession to another costs us close to a thousand dollars and this paperwork is in order to obtain an immigrant quota which allows Kofi to remain in Ghana as a resident investor with me as his dependent.

If you happen to go this route as a couple obtaining your immigration quota/work permits we learned you both can pay for your own quota and no one has to be a dependent. Each independent quota entitles you to bring in a certain number of Diasporas into the country on your quota. No one counsels you well here on the best way to navigate through these processes; everything is by trial and error or after the fact "you should have done such and such." Then of course you pay additional money to do things correctly. "This is Ghana O."

When it was time to go through the immigration madness again we chose to go the route of going out of the country and come back into Ghana which would give us another three or six months to stay in the country legally. This was during the time when money was low because of the building going on, and my health wasn't good I guess due to the stress of these government deadlines.

I had to start using a cane again because my right knee wouldn't allow me to fully bear weight on it. To save money rather than spend money to buy an ace bandage I just tied a piece of cloth around it. Off we went to take a bus to Togo and spend a night, come back the next day and prayerfully return with a six month stamp in our passport.

We got to the Togo border and found out we needed a visa to cross-over. We didn't do our research well and no one ever mentioned the visa which cost $20.00 for each of us but this was the money we were going to use to spend a night in a hotel.

Kofi obtained our visas while a customs officer said I could sit with him and wait for Kofi to return, seeing that I wasn't walking well. The custom officers on the Togo side were caning the people in line and taking whatever they wanted from people's suitcases

When Kofi returned there was a gentleman with him who said he would show us how to maneuver our way in and out between the two boarders so we could go back home the same day now that there was no money for a hotel. We did get our passports stamped on the Togo side and we came back over to Ghana side and took our bus back to our sister Aggie and Nana Edmond's home in Tema.

These bus rides were long and tedious and not pleasurable for me at all. With a three hour ride to Accra and then another two to three hours to Togo; I was not a happy camper. Kofi didn't want to drive for this trip and he didn't feel comfortable driving in Accra just yet.

I would make sandwiches to take with us and we'd buy drinks and hopefully find a decent "place of convenience" which is another name for a toilet. Once home we thought it was worth it until we went to the Cape Coast Immigration office to show our passports.

We were told it looked as if we snuck back into the country because our passports were not stamped as we came back in on the Ghana side. They should have been stamped going out of Ghana, stamped going into Togo and stamped leaving Togo and stamped again re-entering Ghana.

Do you not know we had to travel back to Togo to come into Ghana again to get our passports properly endorsed! The gentleman who led us around didn't lead us correctly and we paid for our learning with a second long trip.

At times I feel as an Afrikan-American as though there is no place for me. I feel like a ping pong ball being bounced back and forth between America and Afrika and wanted by neither. I felt like crying my God, my God, why has thou forsaken me? Spirit spoke to me "if this is all it takes to make you collapse-indeed your faith is small."

All I have to do is look across the shore to the slave dungeon to think about trials of life, suffering and endurance. Since spiritually I am not of this world help me to make myself at home wherever I find myself. Forgive me Lord. Thank you for all you've done for us and all you are doing in our lives. It is always better to face life on the positive tip than the negative, being human I forget at times. Our cup is half full, not half empty.

Lo and behold an astonishing call came through from the Department of Interior /Immigration Enforcement. I was shaking in my boots wondering what have we done or haven't done now? We were invited by Mr. Moses K. Gymfi to come to Accra for a discussion on why it was taking us so long to get our permanent resident papers. We were here almost three years now and still going to immigration every six months to get our passports stamped to stay in the country.

When we met him in his office he was a very sincere man who genuinely wanted to assist us to be in the country legally. He felt we should have at least moved to a status of only applying to immigration once a year.

We explained how we had no cooperation from Barclays Bank to give us our statement of accounts showing how much money we had invested since our arrival in the country. This was holding us up and we needed that paperwork for (GIPC).

The bank branch in Cape Coast would only blame the Accra main branch for the delay. We told him we would stop at the bank in Accra while we were there to ascertain the problem. Of course when we did this the bank manager in Cape Coast became insulted and said we went over his head to complain about him.

Mr. Moses. K. Gymfi was also willing to make some calls for us to enable us to meet our deadlines in a timely manner. He loved our story of repatriation and was impressed with our love for the country and vowed to help us. He was saddened that I had to go through these difficulties while I wasn't ambulating well. He has been one of our true friends here in Ghana ever since we met. One of The Lords' angels sent to steer us in the right direction.

The officers we dealt with in the immigration offices of Accra were found to be considerate and helpful by contrast to the way we were received in Cape Coast. Kofi and I also made friends with the officers in the KEEA district of Elmina and tried to avoid the troublesome Cape site altogether.

With God on our side and a good friend like Mr. Gymfi in our corner we completed all the paperwork with GIPC and received our investment quota/visa. We were finally able to a obtain one year resident permit, then two year permit visas with immigration. Only the fees were increasing yearly to the point we were considering filing for indefinite resident status or the right to abode which we could apply for after residing in Ghana seven years and cost $1,500.00. The best part about this status is we'd never have to visit the immigration office again there'd be no expiration date. The agent said we'd be just like Ghanaians but unable to vote.

God gives nothing to those who keep
Their arms crossed.
African Proverb

Honorable House Of Chiefs

My love had an artist paint an ocean scene on our wall at the hotel and said Adjoa you will have your ocean front one way or another. It's a lovely picture of a beach, with ocean and palm trees that makes me happy every time I look at it.

Time was marching on and the matter of our ocean front land still had not been settled. We've given the sizeable cash deposit. We've been displaced from the land by government officials. We've written letters to everyone we think could help and received no response.

Kofi was weary of going to meetings with the chief and going in circles. I would not give up because I knew that the Creator had a piece of ocean front land somewhere with my name on it. I attended meetings with other Afrikan-Americans facing the same situation and Kofi stayed at home.

Finally I was counseled by a family member (another one of Gods' angels) to take the matter to the House of Chiefs for mediation. We were a bit afraid about going there not knowing the ramifications of this action.

At the same time we read in the newspapers where defrauders had been reprimanded (jailed) for the same amount of money we had given up as a deposit for the land. So this was not a small thing. We however did not want to get tied up in the court system because it's not unusual to go for ten or more years without ever resolving your case. We didn't want to let it go either. So with trepidation we filed our complaint believing we'd have a good outcome and that God would fight for us because we had wronged no one.

In our letter as returnees to our chosen homeland, we expressed our dismay at being swindled out of money. We didn't like being ignored and we wanted restitution. We argued not for ourselves alone but also for the other Afrikan-Americans whom we knew were in the same plight by these same people.

One brother still living here had given up and moved on to another area but we also mentioned him and another couple with children. We asked would the extortion against brothers and sisters ever end! Here we are "*500 years later*" facing the same larceny of heart by leaders who know better. We explained the situation in detail and said all we wanted was two plots of oceanfront land for the amount of money we've already paid.

We received a letter back from the council's secretary saying our complaint was received and a meeting would be called for all parties involved to show up to have their say. Kofi and I went to the House of Chiefs in Cape Coast on the appropriate day and time that we were given and met with their representative.

None of the town's people, elders, nor did the chief arrive. We were told we would be contacted at a later date. Some stakeholders in the town told us that we didn't show up to the meeting the day and time they were given. It seems we were both given different dates, and town representatives asked us to withdraw our complaint and then they would give us our land.

Kofi and I didn't trust them at all but against our better judgment we wrote a letter stating that the chief, the elders, the surveyor and all responsible parties have assured us that if we withdraw the complaint they will surely give us our oceanfront plots of land.

The next correspondence from the House of Chiefs stated that with the complaint withdrawn, the village officials should deal with us speedily and honestly and prayed we would not have to return to them again.

The chieftaincy system is respected in Ghanaian society but may be losing some of its authority as the central government expands its jurisdiction. At the grassroots level (village) the chiefs still perform a wide range of social-economic functions and are venerated by their subjects.

I was even asked to be a queen-mother (Ohemaa) but I declined because I realized the great responsibility that comes with the territory which is mostly financial because of all the community development to be done. I will willingly do all that I can to uplift as many people as I can in my immediate locale but without the title of queen. Quite a few Afrikan-Americans have accepted the honor.

Finally the surveyor and some elders took us along with other brothers and sisters who had been wronged around to see various plots of land and had the nerve to save the oceanfront land for last. When we asked, why did you save the beach land for last?

They responded you may have liked another land even better and chose a different piece of land. No way! We all took the three different plots that were on this beautiful hill Kofi and I call Promise Land. We have a faithful Creator! Just like in the Old Testament when the Hebrew's were going for the land of milk and honey they had to fight for it, it was not handed to them on a silver platter. Praise Him from whom all blessings flow for allowing us to see His salvation. Halleluiah! Sing choir!

Take a stroll along the beach in the beautiful weather.
Perfect place for you-if you need to get it together
Song: Ghana Emotion
Omar

28

Thank You For Our Inheritance!

We were so happy, wow a dream fulfilled. Isaiah 57: 13 KJV, "He that put his trust in me shall possess the land, and shall inherit my holy mountain." Kofi got started building immediately. As a group of three to live in this area we collectively paid and had the land bulldozed and cleared so we could see exactly what we had to work with. Kofi had our building plans drawn long ago; we only had to renew the work permit.

The masons were hired, the foundation was dug, and the profile of the house was laid. Here cement is joined with sand and water and mixed up, poured into molds that make cement blocks one at a time, and each bag of cement makes about 25 strong blocks.

Problems arise when you don't know how much sand was used to make the blocks. If the sand was too much and the cement too small you'll have weak blocks and a weak building. You also cannot watch them work every minute of the day, and undoubtedly bags of cement go missing.

We've been told of stories of employees building their own home while building their client's house with the client's supplies. I wish I kept better records on how much was actually spent to build the house which took about five years to finish due to the dispute.

I was so proud of my beloved who completely immersed himself in his work, all the time saying "I'm doing this for you Adjoa. I don't want you beholden to anyone." He made himself the contractor over this job and bought hardhats for all the workers, kept the worksite neat, and we documented stages of the construction with photos.

He was always a hand's on person and busied himself working with wood or cement, hammering or designing something. I loved coming to the site with Kofi on this beachfront project, we'd have our cooks bring food for all of us on many occasions. We had a battery operated radio playing music and made the worksite a happy place. This was the manifestation of a dream coming true.

It is not easy to manage this work when you're acting as the foreman and you also have to leave the laborers to go and purchase supplies. Many things are done incorrectly by the time you return and many items are missing. We had arches in front of the house, an open veranda facing the ocean, but when we returned the mason had blocked in the arches fully, we couldn't see anything but cement blocks. What in the world were you thinking? He said maybe we would want to hide, (meaning we don't want to be observed). No we are not hiding from anyone, take the blocks out now! We want to see the ocean, sun and blue skies. I say to J.K. our mason you're forgiven. Frequently, the artisans take poetic license and build your house they way they would like it and not as the plans dictate.

We hired an elder from a certain church in the town to be a security guard and watch our building supplies at the site. He was hired to be at the house from six p.m. in the evening until 6a.m. the next morning and was really being paid to sleep. Kofi didn't believe he was going to work because he said nothing would be disturbed or out of place as if anyone were ever there. So we put a log book there for him to sign nightly to report any situation that might arise.

A day before pay day I decided to take a taxi up to the house at 4am. When we arrived at the site no one was there. The taxi driver and I waited until 6a.m. then here comes the guard walking up the hill. As soon as he saw me sitting there waiting him he sat down on the ground and put his hands on top of his head for a long time. Then he came up to me and said he'd just take his personal items away.

He knew he sacked (fired) himself and I didn't have to say a word. I repeated this same investigation and fired another person who was to work in the night securing our building supplies like cement, iron rods, wood boards, tools, water, etc. but they sleep at home at night and come to the job early morning, slipping in and looking for their pay.

I had an idea at the last minute to place a balcony over our bedroom and Kofi designed steps to go up and it was not an easy task to add this after-the-fact with the building plans drawn already. We drove around looking at other peoples' balconies to get ideas. I didn't want a spiral staircase because I'd get dizzy and I didn't trust my footing going up and down.

Kofi said they only way to make the balcony was to place the steps going up pass our bedroom window and I'd lose some of the picturesque view. I told him to go ahead because it would be worth it. The first flight of steps came crashing down one day Kofi came home to tell me. He said they had to be redesigned sturdier with iron rods and a support beam added. Thank God no one was hurt.

Our carpenter calculated the amount of roofing sheets we needed and we called ahead to get the price and saved our money. After about two months we drove off to Accra to pick them up and brought them home for him to install. By the time he finished all the roofing sheets there was still a big opening in the center of the house. Then with all the money spent we had to wait until we could accumulate enough money to purchase the remainder roof sheets to close that big gap. After many rainy days the Lord provided the additional roof sheets, so just buy a few extra sheets to be safe.

Also we found many times we wanted to accomplish a goal but the finances were not at hand and this was frustrating for us but mainly for the workers who can't work if there are no supplies and you risk losing them to leave you for another job elsewhere. As it was they hardly show up when they said they would. We were building as fast as our pensions would take us. Sometimes we could meet payroll but could not buy supplies or vice versa. It was not easy at all but we are at last staying in the part of the house that was finished.

I'm leaving out all the blow by blow knock-out drag-out conflicts between the start and the finish of this house, sometimes even between Kofi and me because when money got short so did patience when we couldn't finish a project as fast as we'd like to. I refused to have us run up a lot of credit the way we did building the hotel. I was not going to have people coming to our house, knocking on our doors at 6a.m. and looking for money we may not have. We had been there and done that and I wanted no repeat of it.

We really lost plenty of money by being overcharged for things and from the theft of a lot of supplies. We had acquired a couple of business loans when building the hotel but the interest was a prohibitive 36% and we weren't going that route again either I insisted to Kofi. This time around we would pay as we go to finish this house, and every month we'd do the little we could do.

Reluctantly we did have to make a couple of bank loans in order to get a large amount of supplies to keep the workers busy but then we'd have problems with their payroll due to the bank payment also due, and the guesthouse was still not taking in enough to pay for the utilities and payroll. It was a very tight budget for a few years but to build a dream takes extreme sacrifice.

Finally our living room, kitchen, dining room, office and bedroom were tiled, painted, and furnished. Kofi purchased the pots, pans, dishes, glasses, silverware, and pictures; kitchen and dining room sets have been made, the living room set was remodeled and looking good. It was only the guestrooms that were unfinished and they would be easy to complete compared to what had been accomplished.

We didn't have piped water yet but we had a water storage container and send for the water delivery truck to fill it which cost about fifty dollars in cedis. We needed a much larger container so the water could last longer before having to refill. Water can't be piped up hill for us because the pressure is too low.

We're using candles and a gas light until the electricity was turned on. We mainly came up on the weekends and kept asking ourselves was this real? We sat on the veranda and watched Gods' creation, the sunrise, sunset, the blue sky, the ocean waves coming in and going out as if it breathes, the birds singing and flying overhead and we said to ourselves' like Louis Armstrong "What a Wonderful World."

What an accomplishment my man has achieved and I could tell he was satisfied and so thankful to have been given the strength to see it through. He was seventy-seven years old at the time. Every day he woke up with determination and went to bed with satisfaction from staying true to his vision. He pushed himself and remained focused in his labor of love building our dream house and he always thanked God as his enabler; whom he said without Him he could do nothing.

All Praise's to the Lord our Maker who has ordained this, maybe even since we were in our mothers' womb.

"When suffering knocks at your door and
You say there is no seat for him, he tells you
Not to worry because he has brought his own stool."
Chinua Achebe

Kofi Are You Leaving Me?

I need to talk more about the medical challenges we've faced here. Most hospitals cannot be compared to those on the other side. They don't have the resources, the staffing, nor do they have the quality of care. I've seen the cleanliness and environmental conditions deteriorate in a particular hospital since I've been here. Frequent electric shutoffs and water shortages don't help either.

Many good doctors are here from Cuba to assist because so many of Ghana's physicians have left the country. Dr. Morna whom we liked in particular was very competent but he'd traveled out of the country for further training. He was usually on duty when Kofi had those hypoglycemic bouts to the emergency room.

Dr. Ghartey managed to care for Kofi and me at his private hospital but thank God I was always treated as an out—patient. I tell everyone just stay well and do your best not to have to have to be admitted to the hospital. Eat well, stay in balance, work, play, exercise, get your rest and keep your immune system built up.

We washed with anti-bacterial soaps to try to avoid skin rashes which may come from perspiring in the hot weather. We kept antibacterial ointment with us at all times to apply to any insect bite because we invariably found ourselves itching and scratching.

Once I made myself sick by scratching and infecting myself with my own dirty hands. I learned my lesson well and it never happened again. We've learned about the herbal remedies growing all around used for various ailments. One good thing is the cost of care here is nowhere near what it would cost in the USA. A week's stay in the hospital here would equal the cost of a onetime doctor visit over there.

Although costs are rising, I recommend signing up for the National Health Insurance Scheme and this will bring costs down even more in the event you find yourself in the hospital. Recently there are several private hospitals opening in Accra that we hear are state of the art, so improvement is on the way.

The first two to three years I caught malaria nearly every month, so much so I once said if I catch it one more time I'm leaving. (You see I didn't mean it.) Everyone's system is different, and even in America the mosquitoes loved me and the repellants never worked for me.

Believe it or not there are some Ghanaians that have never had malaria before. I believe keeping your immune system strong is the key. My big sister Aggie is over sixty years old and recently had malaria for the first time in her life. I had to learn how the symptoms affect me and take the medicine quickly before it makes me weak. My hands start to ache, I feel listless, and may get headache and sore throat. I'll immediately take Fansidar and Artesunate together because the malaria strain has to be double-teamed to rid it from the system.

We haven't tried the new drugs being pushed on the market and we didn't want to be experimenters. This went on at least for three years and then I stopped taking the medicine recommended from the USA because it didn't seem to be helping me at all. Some drugs on the market are fakes and you never know which is which, you only realize you're taking medicine and not getting any better.

I started taking herbal remedies that we were growing in our yard like lemon grass, nim / neem, bitter leaf and moringa. These leaves can be liquefied to drink or boiled to make teas and are now being sold in powder and capsule form.

Usually you'll find if you allow yourself to get run down, exhausted or stressed out, and your resistance is low you may get malaria. After living here four years going I only seemed to catch it two or three times a year which is a significant improvement from my early years here. We also have to take a de-wormer twice a year.

I am used to the aches and pains from arthritis and hip replacements of which there seems to be only palliative relief and no cure. I've learned to live with pain medicine on a daily basis. During my last doctor visit in the states, after looking at my x-rays the Dr. reported it appeared I'd need revision surgery within five years. Well I'm praying to take these same hip implants with me to heaven. I stopped attending physical therapy at the hospital because I didn't like the sickly environment, rather I joined the gym three days a week to help keep out rigor mortis from setting in while I'm alive. However I believe I'll have to give the aggressive exercise up for a more passive one like Qi Gong.

Thirdly, I was found surprisingly to have hypertension that was stroke level high. I remember so well one Christmas Eve Kofi and I were at the immigration dept. for the fifth time to retrieve our passports and were given some story of how the person who had the key was not in, "go and come." No we will not go and come again; we want our passports today and will not leave without them. Today is Christmas Eve and we want our passport in our hands for Christmas. So we'll wait.

In the hallway a nurse was set up taking peoples blood pressure I asked her to please take mine and she did, I was just doing it to pass the time. My pressure was 220/ 110! Anybody who knows anything about this type of reading realizes I was a walking time bomb. I had no symptoms, I felt fine, I was just angry at the run around we were getting trying to collect our passports. That's why high blood pressure is called the silent killer.

I had to go to the hospital to get a sub-lingual medicine to rapidly bring my pressure down. I previously had low to normal blood pressure readings. Hypertension runs in my family and I could stand to lose a few pounds but this was extremely high. I've never experienced anything like this before. I've been on hypertensive meds for a couple of years and I will do my best to work myself off the meds in the years to come through lifestyle change.

What I'm finding out about myself is my emotions cause the elevation, when I stay calm so does my blood pressure. Finding a balance for me is key because there's no need for me to "set it off" reacting anxiously when business is not completed in my time frame; I'm going to take on the same no worries-no hurry in life attitude of Ghanaians. The life I save could be my own. So keep my passport I don't need it unless I'm traveling anyway.

Kofi my sweetie on the other hand was a smoker since he was ten years old, loved his Star beer which caused him to lose his appetite, then he'd suffer from hypoglycemia and would faint anywhere, anytime. Every three to four months he would get a respiratory infection from smoking which would also bring on the malaria because of his low resistance.

Usually he'd get intravenous antibiotics and vitamins and then be able to drive home the same night. If he enjoyed Star beer too much he'd get dehydrated and faint and have to be rushed to the hospital for IV fluids. Well I can truly say in our nine and half years he passed out no less than two dozen times. We started having the doctor assistant (Nat Ashiagbor) come to the house and administer the intra-venous medications and with my past practical nurse training I could take care of him at home.

It started taking him longer and longer to bounce back from these episodes but Kofi had a strong constitution and will to accomplish his goals. I often wished he used this same determination to stop smoking and drinking but those pleas fell on deaf ears or just led to arguments. We got along fine as long as I didn't approach those subjects. He stopped drinking alcohol for the last five years but said he couldn't do that and also give up smoking because he has to die of something. "I don't chase women or take drugs so just be happy" he'd say. My Kofi was a pistol and his own man. He'd always remind me, "I'm human with faults just like you and everyone else so don't give me any grief please."

My birthday is October 5, and Kofi's is October 7th, we would always have a party and celebrate together. We decided to have the party at the beach house "Promise Land" and combine it as a dedication and open house, and the year was 2008. All our good friends and family were there to enjoy with us. Kofi had on his dancing shoes and partied hearty. It almost seemed to me he felt his work was finished and it was time to let loose and enjoy the fruit of his labor. Any party we went to these days Kofi was on the floor dancing through the night. If I didn't want to dance he'd get another partner. He was filled with bliss. My prayer was also answered that he be allowed to finish his work and enjoy it.

During a period of six weeks Kofi was back and forth to the hospital because he wasn't recuperating from illness, he started losing his appetite. He was getting weaker, and refusing to take liquids by mouth.

He decided to sign himself out of the hospital so I could care for him at home. Dr. Nat came to the house and administered continuous IV fluids for him, but my dear one wasn't getting better. There were a total of forty drips administered to him over this course of six weeks. We had been through this so many times a part of me thought that he'd come through it.

People started coming by the house to see him because he hadn't been out in so long. Kohain, Ruben, Sarah, and Richard Mensah while his wife Joyce tried to get Kofi to eat and fed him like a baby, Nana Prempeh and Gladys, Kojo Bey, Sonia and Byron, George and Wanda Pope from Accra and Malkia all paid Kofi visits at his sick bed and brought items like juice or fruit for him. I never wanted to face the fact that he wouldn't recover.

9th February, 2009, was the worst day he had because of being short of breath, he couldn't sit in the chair ten minutes while I made the bed and he needed to lie down. He didn't want his bath. He saw people in the room that I couldn't see. I asked was he leaving me and he shrugged his shoulders as if to say "I don't know." Friends called and asked could they come by and see him and he said yes to Malkia, Chekesha, Jeff and Shikera. God was sending them.

It was 8pm before friends arrived when Kofi took his rings off his fingers and placed them in my hands and told me I should take him to the hospital. I put on a scripture reading CD to keep us both calm. He loved hearing the book of John read: "In the beginning was the Word and the Word was with God, and the Word was God." I started packing his bag to go to the hospital.

Big Mama (Malkia), Chekesha, Shikera and Jeff came, I called my neighbor Ossman a taxi driver, and Jeff had to carry Kofi to the car because he was too weak to walk. All of them came with me to the hospital and stayed awhile but I told them to go because a part of me is reasoning I'll just be here with him through the night and we'll go home in the morning like so many other times before.

The doctor gave him oxygen but the machine wouldn't work unless I manually held it onto the wall, if I let go it wouldn't work. They even tried to tape it to the wall but the tape wouldn't hold. Kofi was restless and trying to pull the nasal oxygen out of his nose as I tried to hold onto the oxygen tank on the wall, he wanted to take it off and I'm trying to keep it running for him. I was distraught, when he started gasping for air.

I called Ann and Ricky, Kohain and Mable, and Sonia and Byron, and then Malkia, Jeff and Shikera to come back to the hospital because I wasn't sure he would make it through the night but I was hoping against hope. I didn't want to acknowledge death, didn't want it to come in, sit down to make itself welcome. I wasn't ready to look death dead in the face.

Then Kofi said "Jesus" and took what sounded like his last breath. It was a death rattling sound I'll never forget and I screamed for the doctor. He said there's nothing we can do now. I could see his throat opening and closing so very slowly, his eyes were fixed and he stopped struggling. I knew this was the end . . . I grabbed him tight, hugged him and rocked him, whispered in his ear so many things; I cried I love you, I love you, go in peace, let the angels lead you to the throne of grace, God have mercy, and put your hand in Gods' hand. I can't remember all that I said.

I held him till I felt all the life go out of him, I heard a nurse say "you helped him go peacefully." Kofi had stepped out of this life into the next to meet his Maker. I'm left feeling numb and dazed. I couldn't cry anymore. I felt so alone, even though everyone whom I called had arrived at the hospital by then, it was 10:30 pm.

I haven't felt this aloneness since my mother passed away; I wish I were a baby and could crawl into her arms again. Only God knew. Only God could help me put one foot in front of the other to walk out of that hospital without my Kofi. Only God could fill this void I felt. God help me! I screamed and cried inside but there were no tears in my eyes.

How could I be falling apart on the inside yet moving and talking to others on the outside. It was like being split into two, as if I wasn't really present but in the land of denial. This is it! The day that we know will come to all of us, yet when it comes it's such a shock. Even though I could see it coming, I didn't want to believe I saw what I saw. My Kingman is gone. I know the body lying in that bed is not him, yet I still feel I'm leaving him there. What shall I do? This is one of those times I'm brought to my knees in spirit. "Precious Lord Take my hand and help me stand."

"When people care for you and cry for you
They can straighten out your soul"
Langston Hughes

A Traditional Ghanaian Home Going

I went with my brother Ricky and sister Ann to their guesthouse and stayed up all night crying and sending the message out. I sent about twenty text messages because I really didn't want to talk yet. The message read: Sorrowfully, I inform you my husband John Calvin Childs aka Pa Kofi has made his transition to join the ancestors this night 10 pm. Funeral arrangements will be forthcoming. Many people called to get the details so I didn't get much sleep. Kofi's relatives can't come to Ghana at this time and neither can any of mine from America.

The next day many members of my Abanyie family and friends escorted me to the morgue and they tracked down the medical examiner to obtain the death certificate. However, we found out because Kofi was a foreign resident there would have to be an autopsy so that there can be no repercussions from family members outside the country after the burial.

There were so many details, loop holes, and hoops to jump I would have been lost without my family. They knew whom to see, where to go, and they protected me by doing all the leg work and would only bring me in when I had to talk or sign some papers. They wouldn't allow me to go in the morgue because they said the place was overcrowded and some bodies were outside the fridge on stretchers. I didn't want to see them either. The doctor asked if I'd witness the autopsy of my husband. I couldn't but my auntie Leticia did observe it. She said someone should be there to be sure things are done proper and she took pictures with her camera phone. I told her I didn't want to see them.

My Afrikan American family in the Cape Coast, Elmina area all rallied around me, I made my immediate financial need known, and they all quickly responded and came to my aid. Our pension had come and all the bills were paid by this time-the 10th of the month and the money spent, but now I needed to make financial deposits on some things required for the funeral.

So many calls were coming through both local and international that I couldn't remember them all and had to get a book to start writing them down. The love and care that poured out from all quarters was heartwarming and strengthening to my Spirit. He was well liked by many. Anyone who didn't like Kofi would have to be because of his strictness. He would tell anyone what he stood for and also the things he wouldn't stand for and then end by saying he hoped he hadn't offended anyone.

Kofi frequently spoke of wanting a traditional Ghanaian funeral and that's what he would have. How many times have people heard him say "my bones will be buried here" as he placed his hand over his heart; too numerous to mention? I've decided to make the weekend of 6th March which was also Independence Day for Ghana the weekend of his funeral.

Oh this is so fitting for Kofi because we were to arrive in Ghana on Americas' Independence Day and now he's obtained his true spiritual independence. We both enjoyed the independence celebrations here because there'd always be vintage movie clips of Osagyefu President Dr. Kwame Nkrumah on television. I knew Kofi loved this.

One day I'd stay at home to receive visitors and the next day I would go to the family house to discuss our "to do" list. Ann had given me a preliminary list of items required: mortuary fees, casket, hearse, undertaker, pastor, cemetery fees, linguist fee, rental chairs, posters, obituary programs, drummers, photographer, Kofi's outfit, my three outfits, room decorations, souvenirs, food and drinks for three days activities, call the American Embassy, go to vital statistics and Cape Coast Municipal Assembly. What could I do without my dear sister Ann?

My first night sleeping alone in our room was very restless for me. The second night I talked out loud as if Kofi could hear me. I said Kofi where are you? How is it where you are? I didn't hear his voice but I felt a warmth envelope me and a inner knowing, I really can't explain how it comforted me " I'm like the positive energy you feel all around you." I've slept soundly ever since and have moved over to sleep on the side where he used to sleep, wearing his bedroom slippers, and spraying his cologne on my pillow.

Every morning one dear mother in the village named Maame Pola would be sitting outside my front door waiting for me to get up. When I open my door she is sitting outside waiting to check on me and see that I'm okay. She speaks no English and I can't carry on a conversation in Fante, but we get along fine and seem to understand each other. I can always call for one of the girls to translate for me. She taught me to respond Ya Henewa when she greets me, which is to acknowledge her in return as the chiefs' daughter.

Maame Pola, Kofi and I had a joke that she was his second wife because she would always plead with him to stop smoking. She stayed close to me until Kofi was buried. Her church choir came one evening to sing gospel songs to encourage me and it was so soothing to my soul. A gathering of friends were with me that night and took me by the hand to stand and do a praise dance and clap to show that God was with me and has not left me alone; that I should not act like someone who has no help or no hope. God is near so praise Him and surrender Kofi over to His will. I did my best.

Maame Pola brought me sea water to bath with which is part of the customary widows' rights. She wanted me to wear herbs and tie a key around my waist to prevent Kofi from coming back and try to have physical relations with me or harass me in any form but I refused. Kofi never forced himself or harassed me in life and he surely wouldn't do it in the afterlife.

Another night our Ghanaian friend Ambassador and his culture group called the Back House came to perform; they said to help Kofi's Spirit find his way to the ancestors. There's a place deep inside us that only the drum can touch and Kofi loved drums so it was appropriate. Many of the village residents came around to sit with me and encourage me on this night too. Kofi and I stood in at Ambassadors' wedding in place of his wife Mimi's parents who could not make it in from Atlanta. It was an honor to do that for Dr. Andoh and Maame Kali.

Meanwhile big Brother Tony Abanyie was home from New Jersey and was helping me write the program and obituary, and Mr. Aggrey Fynn was checking at the mortuary, doing the administrative leg work so I didn't have to run here and there. He's an angel assigned to me. There was a death extract form, a pink slip that had to be obtained to take to the embassy which was also needed to get the burial permit.

Mr. Moses K. Gymfi the Assistant Director of Immigration in Accra and his entourage were in the area and made a courtesy call to offer their condolences. Friends Pastors Jack and Sylvia Gardner of Crusaders for Christ Ministries, also in from Accra stayed with me for two days and paid for souvenirs with Kofi's and my picture on it.

Gladys has come down our driveway wailing with sadness from Accra, we've known her for seven years, Kofi always called her daughter and she's offered to buy the items needed for Kofi's last bath. These items consist of Dettol antiseptic, Geisha soap, perfume, camphor, Florida Water, shaving razor, nail clipper, new sponge and towels. She said she would also be by my side to assist me during the three funeral days. During the time when we had no money for five months she was one of the angels who brought us foods we like from Koala the store in Accra where foreigners like to shop. She'd bring Kofi's favorites: French bread, boiled ham and cheese.

Numerous e-mails were pouring in from all over and I felt myself being lifted up by the prayers and condolences of many people. I was going through the motion of activities but felt as though I was in a dream. My only peace was at night when I slept and dreamt of Kofi still alive.

I managed to cope one day at a time. People were doing such nice things for me and the Abanyie family told me of so many items on the list that they would be financially responsible for starting with the purchase of the casket. We've estimated the costs of the funeral to be between five and six thousand Ghana Cedis. The emotional support they provided was even more precious to me.

From America my sisters Nia and Renee and her husband Alfred, Cousin Linda and my son Latif along with friends Leej and Netfa Harold, Nancy Fairley, Kwame Fordjour, and Bayhtia had sent financial donations and moral support. Most of the adults in the Abanyie family that live outside of Ghana supported with a hundred dollars each.

Auntie Essie (A Ghanaian lady who reminds me of Rosa Parks) whom Kofi and I made her acquaintance in Barclays Bank four months before he passed has brought me black material that she plans to make an outfit for me to wear. Mrs. Mary Brown had cooked food and driven all the way from Accra to present it to me to be sure I was eating. Mr. Asare of Ghana Broadcasting Company offered a free advert on the television for Kofis' obituary but I decided against it because it would probably bring in more people than I could feed. I was truly grateful for the kind gestures shown by all.

Imakus had written a letter to the Hoteliers Association to inform them of Kofis' transition and they have responded with a sizeable donation. I lacked for nothing (except my Kofi) and I experienced what it means to know "The Lord is my Sheppard." He was surely moving through all these wonderful people.

I traveled to Accra, the Capital of Ghana to the American Embassy to complete the necessary paperwork for "Death of an American Citizen in a Foreign Country." I handed over copies of the Ghanaian paperwork in order to get the American version of a death certificate. It was Friday and I had to stay over the weekend and pick up the 21 copies they'd issue on Monday. Gladys' Ezes' friends Uncle Roland and his wife Agnes graciously offered us their home for the night.

Saturday, I visited over night with Albie and Rose and they took me to the new Accra Mall, out to dinner at Chez Afrique and met some of their friends from Pram Pram; it was an uplifting day. Sunday was spent with Pastors Jack and Sylvia who escorted me back to the embassy on Monday morning.

Once back in Cape Coast Monday afternoon I met with the undertaker Mr. Quarshie. He tried to reassure me not to worry and that he'd do a good job. Still I can note too many times folks don't look like themselves at their funerals and I didn't want that for my Kofi. I requested his arms be folded across his chest just like he slept; and not straight down at his sides so unnaturally.

Mr. Quarshie told me to pack three pairs of traveling clothes for Kofi to have for his journey. These would be placed in the bottom of the casket under him. It made me chuckle but I complied and packed some of Kofis' favorites. The suit he liked, two other outfits, his Obama hat, his glasses, watch, belt and hankies. They also add a few cedis to pay the fare to cross the river. (Traditional Ghanaian Funeral)

Auntie Araba and Shankus (Cool Running, Mr. Aggrey Fynn) went to the cemetery and picked out the burial plot. I'd later inspect the burial site but was not to attend the burial per custom. Widows don't attend their husbands burials here, it's felt the burden is too much to take. I am okay with this because it's one part of the funeral service I've never liked, watching the casket being lowered into the ground. Kofi's spirit has already transcended and he's not in that coffin.

When I inspected the burial site I liked where it was situated not far from the road, under a tree, with a valley view. The one thing I didn't like was the plot next to his appeared only three inches apart. I wanted to have that plot but was told even if I pay for it no one will know anything about it when I'm gone; even if there is a receipt someone will already be buried in the plot I've paid for. Pre-payment of burial plots are not done in Ghana.

I curiously checked cremation prices which have skyrocketed over the years we've been here from hundreds of cedis to thousands of cedis. I did learn if you join the Cremation Society your cost could be lowered substantially. I was only curious and not intending one for Kofi.

I was spared so much of the hassle of pulling this ceremony together by all the love that was pouring out to me that before I knew it it's time to move to the family house for the three final days. Friday is the usual wake-keeping day. However I asked for no wake-keeping but that Kofi would lay in-state at the family house for close family and friends who may stop by.

Auntie Leticia hired a choir for the Friday night gathering. Saturday would be the funeral at Zion Methodist Church, burial at Asokyeano Cemetery thereafter and the re-pass at the banquet hall at the family house. Sunday was the thanksgiving church service. I also had to be thinking of a forty day ceremony within the next twelve days that is part of the traditional Ghanaian funeral.

The next traditional ceremonies are for the one year, five year, ten year, twenty and so on. As long as I'm alive I'll choose to remember him, as I told Kofi not even death will separate us. Some folks wondered why I didn't have his funeral at our home where he toiled and sweated.

We have a Ghanaian family and when someone dies in the family, that person goes back to their family house for their funeral. The Abanyie family has convinced us long ago that we are part of them, and even while Kofi was alive Ann would say we're going to lay you in-state upstairs in the family house and he agreed. The forty day ceremony will be held at the hotel in Ayensudo and the one year ceremony will be held at our home in Brenu.

So this way all the bases would be covered. I buried Kofi where our family is buried and also where I'll be buried in Asokyeano Cemetery. My soul is satisfied with this. So be it.

On Friday 6th March, 2009, Peter the photographer filmed taking Kofis' body from the morgue in an ambulance to drive to our town of Ayensudo and then to the town of Brenu Akyinim where our home is. The linguist will do some type of rituals for the departed per custom.

I was required to remain at the family house to receive guests and be available for any eventualities that might arise. There were still little details like putting up canopies, picking up 200 chairs, installing outside lighting, cleaning crates of fish, etc. My reason for writing no wake-keeping on the funeral posters was to limit the number of people coming just to be inquisitive and may not be friends of Kofi.

However this night turned out to be a no wake-keeping-wake-keeping. I had to view the layout of the room prior to them bringing his body. It was done majestically in a Kente pattern and lace and flowers, all the walls and ceiling were covered. Wow! Was all I could say!

Then Kofis' body was brought to the family house with additional rituals performed before entering the house. We all wailed as the pall bearers carried his body up the stairs to the viewing room where he'd lay in-state. I delayed going to view his body because I had no idea what he'd look like and I didn't want the last picture in my mind to be something other than my dear one. Sister Aggie felt the same way and didn't go up until Ann came down reporting how well he looked.

The choir was singing soul stirring music, many friends were in and out, a lot of shaking of hands, offering encouragement and everyone who went up to view the body would come down remarking how Kofi looked stately. Everyone was urging me to go up to see him but I waited until 4am to go and be alone with his remains until 6am when the viewing of his body would begin again Saturday morning. Ann said she was pleased at the turnout for the evening. I was watching myself go through the movements like in a movie. I prayed for God's strength.

7th March, 2009 4am Saturday morning I rose up to commune with the spirit of my Kofi. I was amazed to see that his body did look good. He appeared to be sleeping, looked so handsome dressed in white, adorned with gold plated jewelry that made him look like royalty, like a King's Kid. He looked so much like him-self I couldn't even cry. His countenance spoke without uttering a word as if to say do not cry for me "I'm in Perfect Peace."

I wanted to shake him and say wake up, wake up Kofi but rather I began to sing songs of praise to God. Great is thy Faithfulness, It is Well, I Surrender All, Swing Low Sweet Chariot, I Know my Redeemer Lives and many others. I walked around the casket singing for two hours until people began coming to view the body again before the funeral. Then I sat at his feet beside the bed, Gladys came and sat beside me and we hummed hymns until it was time to close the casket and I could not help but fall on Kofi's body as if to get my last hug from him.

Rabbi Kohain Halevi performed the eulogy at the funeral; he and his family are good friends for the past nine and half years and he willingly humbles himself to meet the spiritual needs of our community. Family, friends and acquaintances have packed the church but prior to starting another casket was carried to the front next to Kofi's. My sister Ann informed me we've been asked to allow for a double funeral.

Kohain was then asked to preside over a person's funeral he had never met; and being the diplomat that he is, he handled the situation with poise. His sermon, words of comfort and capsulation of Kofi's life was befitting and spirited. I could at last feel myself coming to terms with surrendering myself to the Omnipotence of God. What else could I do? Until sister Aggie and Joyce brought me to tears as they broke down reading their portion of the obituary.

During the funeral one pastor made an appeal for donations to purchase louvers for the church windows. I've been here long enough to not be surprised by anything that occurs'—even at a funeral (although I want to shout this is a funeral-no commercials please). I remembered attending Ann's mother Mama Marion Bernice Abanyie's funeral-there were five caskets in the front of the church at one ceremony. "This is Ghana."

Ricky found someone to play a bugle at the church and burial which was proper for Kofi's military days and Ann even remembered to get fresh flowers sent and signed them from both our families in America. The family had me rent a "Kufuor bus" (A big municipal 50 passenger bus) to take anyone who needed a ride from the church to the burial site.

While they were gone I was whisked away to the family house for my widow rites. An elder auntie was assigned to me who spoke only Fante, we communicated the best we could. I bathed myself in sea water that she poured over my head without alerting me and I felt I was drowning; before I could fully catch my breath here comes another bucket of water over my head.

There were white beads I had to wear on my wrists and neck to keep evil spirits away. I was doused with talcum powder as she helped to dress me. I was given new earrings to wear and coins to hold in my hand, wave around my head and up and down my body and to throw backwards over my head to the drummers.

I had to eat a plate of mashed egg, palm oil and yam without stopping for any drink, and this was to signify me not to talk of my suffering again. I ate white chicken light soup of which I could eat the meat but not break any bone. If I broke a bone I'd be seen to have had a hand in my spouse's demise. These are some of the myths prevailing concerning death here.

I could then go out and meet all and sundry in a new black and white outfit symbolizing my new life as a cleansed widow, never to wear black again to mourn for my dear deceased husband. As per Ghanaian custom I was free, even free to remarry.

I went out into the crowd where the Fontomfrom drums were loudly beating, the cultural dancers were dramatizing their steps and the caterer's were serving out a buffet of Ghanaian delicacies. Joyce and Richard (also named Kofi and Adjoa) Mensah collected donations. Ann was all over the place making sure everything was done properly, and true family, friends, and well wishers were there to hold me up emotionally.

Precious Kofi's name will come up many a day and he has made his mark in Cape Coast and Elmina as Ann always said. I'm grateful to Ann and all my Abanyie family who have given their all to send Kofi home in a grand traditional Ghanaian style.

Sunday 8th, March 2009 was the thanksgiving church service where we showed our gratitude to God for Kofi's life, for all our lives and for Gods' grace and love to us his children. Church services in Ghana are long, long. There were six offerings collected and I don't know if that was normal or because foreigners were among the congregation that day. Ann and Ricky gave plenty of money in Kofi's name, even for the church windows.

During a special prayer for me the female Rev. Minister snatched the white beads off my neck and wrists the traditionalist auntie had put on me and said "you're free." It was unexpected and startled me but I knew where she was coming from. I didn't need any white beads to ward off any evil spirits because our God is an awesome God, Lord over all!

In the afternoon we all gathered at the family house for a different unexpected ceremony for me. During this ceremony there was discussion regarding which males should be placed at my back to support me in place of Kofi.

Brother Ricky Hooper was elected because he's in close proximity of Cape Coast to me in Elmina. Big brother Emmanuel was chosen as his backup supporter. Both of them had to give an acceptance speech, while Ricky was carried and sat on a stool three times; and I also had to give a speech in acceptance of them. I said some few words and ended with 'odo mouquins" which means I love my two husbands and everyone laughed!

One of the Ghanaian friends present said that Kofi's journey here should be documented. He said that he didn't know of any other Afrikan American who repatriated to Ghana and lived here as a Ghanaian, made his transition here and ended his sojourn with a traditional Ghanaian funeral except W.E.B. Dubois. This man worked for the Ghana television network.

It's customary for the family to ask if there are any debts after the funeral and family members come together to pay off those debts. Halleluiah! There was no one else to pay, there were no debts. In Ghanaian culture if Kofi owed anyone anything, those persons were asked to come forth after the burial, during the funeral rites and if they did not come forth they cannot come once the burial weekend is over. My sister said if someone should come I should send them to my family head if anyone tries it. No one ever came to say that Kofi owed them anything. What a miracle, everything was over and I'm debt free with enough to prepare for the next customary ceremony.

All this really uplifted my spirits and we danced to prove that the good Lord had some-how lightened our load and was beginning to heal our hearts. So we did a dance of praise unto the Lord to the song "Jesus is my strength O, go, go, go, go high." Our mourning was turned into dancing. Psa.30:11 KJV, Our Father had received his own back unto himself.

I would love to stay in the warm cocoon of the family house, but it was time to check to see what was going on in Ayensudo. Bro. Shabazz thoughtfully helped out so the Esteem family could attend the funeral. Owusu and Kwesie our faithful friends and taxi drivers drove the staff back and forth the day of the funeral at no costs which I appreciated. Ann allowed Sammy to transport me everywhere I needed to go in one of her cars and he took me home. I have been held up by so many caring, giving people and underneath me were Gods' everlasting arms.

By the grace of God came Monday morning and I have come through like pure gold, purified in the fire, praising my Savior all the day long. Words cannot express the love and sincere gratitude I have to God, to my Afrikan American family, to one and all who have enabled me to stand strong especially my Abanyie, Steele-Dadzie, Cole and Hooper families for all they have done. I pray God bless everyone who said a prayer, gave an offering, lend a hand or any good deed, bless you a hundred fold for your kindness and I literally felt myself being held up by prayers. This is what friendship and family is all about as Kofi would say: loving, caring and sharing.

I am America, the part you won't recognize
But get used to me. Black, confident, cocky,
My name, not yours, my religion, not yours,
My goals, my own, get used to me.
Mohamed Ali 1975

31

Fortieth Day Ceremony-One Year Memorial For Kofi

It is felt "In Ghana Here" that the departed travel around the world of spirits for a number of days during which they may have to cross rivers, mountains and such and by the fortieth day it is hoped they've found their rest. This is the purpose of the fortieth day ceremony, that at last the deceased has found rest for their soul.

On 21ˢᵗ March, 2009 we had a short sweet program of scripture reading, responsive reading, tributes, singing, culture group, drumming, dancing, poetry, eating and drinking, enjoying the life and memories of my sweetheart. The summer hut was overflowing with family and friends again showering me with peace and love. We prayed that dear Kofi rest well in the bosom of the Most High.

I had to purchase a headstone and build the tomb for the one year ceremony. I had four months to prepare for my husband's one year ceremony. Ann, Mr. Aggrey Fynn and I have been going back and forth to the cemetery with tiles, cement, and money to have the headstone engraved and tomb procured. I gave the cemetery caretakers a deposit to start the work and had to keep returning to see if the work was being done.

Most of the time the work is not done and you have to keep pleading with them to do the work in a timely manner. When the work was finished I spent a little over Thirteen Hundred Ghana Cedis equaling about $1,000.00.

Ann's brother named Francis in New Jersey agreed to purchase a special photograph of Kofi to be placed on the headstone and sent it from the USA. When I questioned him about repaying the cost of this picture (over $300.00) he said "no, aren't we family." So I am giving Mr. and Mrs. Francis and Elizabeth Abanyie my biggest God Bless You from the deepest part of my heart right here and now.

It rained off and on the day of the one year ceremony which was held at Promised Land beach house after we returned from the cemetery and unveiled the tomb. Precious family and friends were present for a tree planting, Holy Communion, calling on the ancestors and libation ceremony in Kofi's honor. Rabbi Kohain stepped in to officiate and I documented it all by video.

The strangest thing happened when Dr. Nana Maame Malkia arrived. The car horn on Kofi's truck kept blowing and wouldn't stop as if to herald her arrival. Kofi was among us. Mrs. Crentstil's caterers, the Back House group singers and some dancing made the day of remembrance special for my dear one.

Time is healing me and the pain in my heart is lessening but "Oh what a mighty tree has fallen." Who can fill this man's shoes? The year has come and gone too fast but thank God I'm still here standing keeping Kofi's memory and our dream alive.

As you can see I have enough bliss to last me a lifetime overflowing from my life with Kofi here in Ghana. Tracy from New York also a widow called to cheer me up when Kofi made his transition. She told me how her deceased husband was still taking care of her even from the grave. She said because of him she knew what love looked like, what love smelled like and she also knew what love was not.

Since she recently married a Ghanaian man named Professor I guess he passed her test. I understand just what she means because I know that I have been loved. Kofi cherished me and showed me by his actions that he loved me. His love just kept on giving, and giving. I look around Promised Land and all I see is love in panorama. Kofi came in to my life to show me how to love. Now that he's gone I can see this 20/20. I have to take what I've seen, learned and practice it myself.

Kofi is still taking care of me from the grave too. I feel his presence all the time, I know he's got my back for the rest of my life and all I have to do now is gratefully enjoy and share my blessings. Can you believe Kofi sent me a present which I received after he passed away!

Moses said Kofi gave him money to purchase me a battery operated shortwave radio for Valentine's Day! Moses gave it to me after Kofi passed. The radio we had was broken, and we listened to the news together over the radio especially when the electricity was shut off. I loved my present and I cried grateful tears. Kofi had a tough rigid exterior but my baby loved me and that's all I've got to say.

My Kofi was a hardworking, generous, respectful, talented and spiritual man. In the funeral obituary I used the acronym MAN and named some adjectives that I ascribed to him:

M=Marvelous, Masculine, Moral, Mentor, Methodical, Mellow (No one knew his mellow side but me.)
A=Able, Aboveboard, Ambitious, Artistic, Authentic, Adorable, Admirable, Anointed
N=Neat, Natural, No Nonsense, Noble, Note-worthy.

There is a poem in a prayer book dear Gladys Eze gave me that confirmed the good feeling I had after I questioned, Kofi two days after he passed. Where are you?

I AM NOT THERE

Do not stand at my grave and weep.
I am not there. I do not sleep.
I am a thousand winds that blow;
I am the diamond glints on snow.
I am the sunlight on ripened grain.
I am the gentle autumn rain.
When you awaken in the morning's hush,

I am the swift uplifting rush.
And quiet birds in circled flight.
I am the soft stars that shine at night.
Do not stand at my grave and cry.
I am not there I did not die.

*

By Elizabeth Frye, 1932

I was given so much peace from the words of this poem. Kofi is energy, love and light now; we are also of the same energy but seen and he is unseen and the vibration and imprint of his essence is unmistakably felt around our properties.

I miss him terribly. Yet everywhere I look around Promised Land I see the essence of him, the places he walked, worked, labored, laughed, lamented, loved, lived life to the full, laid his head, and where the Almighty lengthened his days past three score and ten to seventy-seven. I believe he lived life completely here in Ghana these last nine and half years more than he did in all the sixty-seven years he lived in America. He died a happy man. How many people get to live their dream before they make their transition? He lived life his way. What a blessing!

The following is a quote from our friend Prof. Nancy Lundgren's book Watch and Pray.

"Life is a preparation for death, but death is not the end-it is a new kind of beginning. Death is a part of life. The Sankofa bird is an important Akan symbol. It reminds the Fante that they must keep an eye on what went before, remember from where they come, and recognize that the past is part of the present. In life it is important to be able to look back with grace. Gold or diamonds are not what count. What counts is to be able to look back at a life lived well. When one dies, one must be prepared. One must have one's life in order and must have lived one's life with care. You never know when God will take you, so you must always be prepared. You must always live your life well. You must watch and pray." [2]

---

[2] Watch and Pray, a Portrait of Fante Village Life in Transition by Nancy Lundgren, page 150.

"Change will not come if we wait for some other person
Or some other time; we are the ones we've been waiting for.
We are the change we seek."
President Barak Obama, USA

President And Mrs.Obama Welcome To Ghana!

Before Kofi made his transition we were all so engrossed in the presidential campaign of the USA politics with Barack Obama running for president. Even though Kofi was ill, he and I went to the American Embassy to file our absentee ballots.

Everyone was so excited here in Ghana, even Ghanaians. There seemed to be more excitement here than in America because they were showing on television people who said they weren't going to vote for him over there. Ghanaians we talked to could not understand how an Afrikan in America would ever consider not voting for a "brother" as they put it. "Who wouldn't want to see their brother in the Whitehouse?" The thought was inconceivable to them.

There was no sleep for us the night the ballots were being counted. Kofi was attempting to keep the score of all the states that voted for Obama and we were up until daybreak. When he won! I ran outside to ring a bell.

Our community planned a celebration party when Obama won. We enjoyed ourselves and jubilated over this history making event. The whole country was caught up in the global excitement of another example of one of God's miracles!

Kofi was elated at being alive to see as he said "A black man make it from the outhouse to the Whitehouse" quoting Jessie Jackson from previous years. He felt so privileged to see the day, an Afrikan winning an American Presidential campaign and thanked the Most High and the Ancestors for making what had been thought an impossible dream come to fruition. He shed tears that Afrikan children could look at Barack Obama believing they could achieve anything.

The seat for the Presidency of the United States was thought to never be achieved by an Afrikan. We should have our chance and any other capable person from whatever ethnic group they belong must also have their chance. We had our victory party at Mable's Table where our community often meets. At this party our group decided to plan our own inaugural party to be held in unison with the one in Wash. D.C. and watch the ceremony on big screen television. A time to rejoice!

However when it was time for the inaugural party Kofi was not well and although we paid for our tickets we didn't attend the party, we watched the inauguration at home on the television and Chekesha kept us company.

Well you all know by now that President Obama and his family visited Ghana in July of 2009. There were billboards all around the town with pictures of Pres. Barak Obama and Pres. Mills with the motto: *Partnership for the future* and pictures of President and Mrs. Michelle Obama saying welcome!

The police swat teams were observing from the rooftops, the specially trained canines were sniffing the gutters, the police were hyped up determined to push back the crowd and they were very rude to those of us waiting patiently for him.

We watched the helicopters fly in overhead and screamed when the motorcade made its rounds. All I can say is there was pandemonium of excitement all over Cape Coast.

Ann and I were in the front of the crowd and on television, sitting in front of the castle dungeon awaiting his arrival from 11am until 4pm just to see him wave his hand at the sea of expectant admirers. He wasn't allowed to come close to the crowd at all, just wave from afar.

There were various opinions on what the real purpose of his visit might be. Some folks said it was due to the recent oil find in the country; others said due to Afri-Com military objectives. We may never know the real deal but one sure thing, we had reason to be euphoric; the first Afrikan-American President of America landed on Ghana's soil.

It was mentioned that Mrs. Michele Obama traced her Afrikan roots to Cape Coast. So of course we claim her as part of our Central Region, Cape Coast family too.

Let Go And Let Ghana

This chapter is made of short stories depicting daily life in Ghana. It was not easy to make the necessary adjustments. Yet I learned to bend and not break and go with the flow without losing my sense of self. I added some funny stories and we'd do better to laugh things off and be light hearted as many Ghanaians are. I've also included short stories about things that made me very happy along with stories of some things that still amaze me.

Obroni
When we first arrived here little children would walk by saying Obroni how are you? Obroni give me money? Obroni this, Obroni that, so finally we asked some Ghanaians what does this mean? One person said it meant white person and I cried literal tears. I could not believe we've came this far "home" to be called a white person. This caused me much sadness for too long.

Something has to be done I exclaimed to teach the children that we are their mothers, fathers, sisters, brothers, aunties, and uncles who have come home. We were still questioning this to others who said oh it just means foreigner or one who doesn't speak the local language; one who has come from across the sea. I would try to teach the children who understood English that I'm also an Afrikan.

I found out the proper word that should be used for those of us returning from the Diaspora is Ababio-One who has returned; also the word Bibini which means black, "me Bibini." This is how I would answer now when called Obroni to teach the children. I learned not to let it get me upset any longer because I know who I am, an Afrikan who has returned home to her mother continent. There is a lot of re-education needed to build the bridge between us and our Ghanaian brothers and sisters. They would also stare at us so intensely and so long, just looking ahh.

Tomorrow

It didn't take long to find out when someone tells you I'll come tomorrow, or I'll see you tomorrow—they don't really mean the next day. Most of the time folks will not come as you expect them to but will show up when you don't expect them. You can hire a laborer or a repairer who says they will report to work the next day; and you may delay your schedule to wait their arrival, but they may not show up. You can call them the next day and they'll say they are coming, but they may not show up and string you along for weeks saying "Tomorrow I will come."

At times they've gone on to accept jobs from other people or to finish previous jobs. We still can't understand why can't yea be yea and nay—nay. So we're told by many friends "This be Ghana." Tomorrow really means whenever I decide to get back to you. Too many tell you what you want to hear but not meaning a word they say. It seems to me that they don't want to disappoint by telling the truth so they'd rather mislead you. Maybe they behave this way because jobs are hard to come by. Recently I was told *I'm coming* means they are busy.

*

We never like to turn people away who come to us for work. We would rather find something for the person to do because they came to us seeking and this is one of the reasons why we are home to help. This has brought various experiences into our lives. People may come who only want to work for one month to get enough money to travel, but they'll never disclose this. They just leave.

One young man came to say he'd do anything, he just wants some work. He said he had farming knowledge so we hired him to plant us a garden. He went right to work tilling the ground, testing the soil, writing his notes of the list of items to buy, fertilizer, seeds, tools and such. We were too trusting and should have purchased the items ourselves but we gave him the money to shop and we never saw him again. We've found out it's the ones who say "Oh I will stay with you always" are the ones quickest to leave.

*

When we first arrived in Ghana the rate of pay for the unskilled worker was one dollar a day. Over the years things are improving to where the minimum wage is between three and four dollars in Ghana cedi equivalent a day for the untrained laborer. Civil service and trained workers are paid better but still low in average to the western world.

A teacher may only receive two hundred Ghana cedis equaling about $150.00 a month. When venturing out you have to keep money handy to give out because you'll surely be asked by people on the street for donations for food, drink or any such reason.

I see in the news now that Ghana is one of the new emerging economies moving into a middle class status. I still see a big divide between the rich and poor here with prices rising frequently in the markets and gasoline is equal to $5.00 per gallon. Keep blessing us so that we can be a blessing to others is our prayer without ceasing.

Not Taking Responsibility

Many times if there's an altercation between a foreigner and a Ghanaian and the Ghanaian is in the wrong, they will never admit it because it involves a non-Ghanaian. After all it's believed the foreigner can afford to pay for any damages. Someone hit our truck from behind and we both pulled over. We were not at fault if we're hit from behind but the other driver jumped out shouting in Fante and drawing a crowd and everyone began to have something to say.

We didn't know what was said but everyone was loud and raising their hands, we wind up giving the other driver GHC10.00 just to get away from the crowd and we were hit from behind. Our truck was not damaged and neither was his, we allowed the crowd to intimidate us.

We didn't call the police because it gets too involved and you wind up going to court to settle and the average person cannot pay the repairs and court fees. It would really be a waste of time and money for us.

At another time while at the fitter (auto mechanic) a driver backed his car into the passenger side of our truck. This time it was an honorable man who took us to his mechanic and paid to have our car repaired. Thank you Mr. Agama, so it's not all bad.

*

More excitement as we're driving and Kofi hit a goat on the highway and pulled over; didn't the whole village run out screaming when they know the owner of the goat is supposed to keep his goats penned or tied up. Yet this is another time we end up paying just to get away from a rowdy crowd.

*

Then there was a van driver attempting to make a U-turn on our roadside and he backed into our fence and broke it. I grabbed my video camera to document the accident and as the driver was still navigating the turn he hit the fence again. I yelled at him to stop ruining our fence and he yelled back at me "are you a Ghanaian, go back to your own country." Kofi told him to get down from the van and pay some cedis to fix the fence.

We could see that he was drunk driving and surprisingly the persons riding on the van with him also told him to pay us. We happily received GHC10.00 from him before he went on his way still fussing that we should go to our own country. We told him if he knew his history he'd know that is just what we did.

*

Also if your employee spoils your merchandise, wrecks your car, or breaks anything they cannot pay for it; they just don't have the money. GHC500.00 of repair work was completed on the truck preparing for the arrival of my son and my best friends visit. We wanted them to be able to drive problem free. However one of our employees went on and errand for us and made an unlawful U-turn and hit a taxi causing another GHC500.00 damage to the taxi and our truck the day before their arrival.

We were sick but thankfully sisters Ann and Aggie came to the scene of the accident and had us all go directly to her mechanic to solve the problem, we could do nothing but immediately repair both vehicles because our driver was at fault. The taxi had to be speedily repaired to get back on the road to make money for the owner; or we'd also be charged with paying for the missed daily sales.

Our employee could not afford the repairs but did offer to work for free for the amount of money we had to pay. Since this was his second car accident we decided to cut our losses and terminate his employment.

*

You would not believe as I'm writing this I heard a loud crash outside my window. I went to look and see two young men who were riding on a homemade wagon called a man truck that had obviously run amuck down our driveway and crashed into the fence, breaking it and our sign board down. I told the guys they have to buy some wood and some nails to fix it.

I called my right-hand man Moses to come and see what happened. As they say here "wonders will never end." This young man named Kwesie came immediately with a 2x2 wood board and some 3 inch nails for the repairs. My faith was restored I've learned not to generalize.

Dummy Up
When our employees do something wrong and we question them, they stand right in front of us and won't say a word. They look here and there and no matter how we keep asking what has happen, or who did such a thing; they will not answer.

Also our culture is different whereas we want our children to look us in the eye when we speak to them. In this culture children look down and to look the elder in the face is disrespectful. Also very rarely will they tell on one another. It seems they would all rather be punished together than to report the wrong of a coworker.

*

Many will answer "What" when asked a question or if they didn't understand what was asked. I could never answer "what" to my parents. I find it offensive and ask them to respond better by saying that they didn't hear me well.

Customer Service

I know I wouldn't be the only one to say that there is a lack of good customer relations in the service industry and it could well be improved upon. Many times you enter a small retail store and first you have to wake up the salesperson or their attitude is such that you feel as though you are a bother to them to enter their store to make a purchase.

I have often walked out of a store after the person working there refused to even greet me and acknowledge my presence, nor respond to my greeting and I've come to spend money with them. Then there's the squeezing of the face and the sucking of the teeth some do so well, which causes me to immediately walk out the store.

Also instead of taking your money and completing your order, the salesperson will leave you to begin waiting on another customer who has entered the store after you arrived. It's not even common to hear a thank you after spending money with some merchants. It seems the merchant feels he's doing the seller a favor. The customer feels they are doing a favor by purchasing goods, yet one hand washes the other as the proverb goes here. Each one must appreciate the other.

Once I commented to a sales owner that I had come into her store so often but never saw her smile; she immediately responded with the biggest smile. Thereafter when I came to shop she was all smiles and would converse with me and we have become very friendly. When Kofi passed she offered a sizable donation and even allows me to credit items if the need arises. Thank you to the Araba T Ventures family.

*

Kofi and I always tried to instill self-esteem in the various laborers and repairers who worked for us so to instill some pride in themselves and the work they do. Kofi would tell them that their work was their signature which lived on after they've left our premises; telling them that if they work well we'd be glad to refer them to our friends requiring the same work.

It can be risky recommending artisans to others because sometimes people are not consistent in their behavior. They may work well for you and when you refer them to someone else they behave differently or won't work as well. It has happened.

So far we're only able to recommend one carpenter Abeku and one plumber Atta. This is not to say that some of the other persons craft wasn't good but their character left a lot to be desired or they wanted to literally rob us with their high prices, and many times the work is done haphazardly with no thought to the finished product.

Robbed In Town

Kofi and I just left the bank and drove a block away, parked and got out to shop. He went to the left to buy eggs and I was looking at some shoes on the right side of the street. There's a crowd of people all around me pushing their shoes at me to buy. Kofi sent a crate of eggs to the car by a young lady. I sat my bag down to push the car seat up and place the eggs on the back seat, and that fast someone picked up my bag.

All the money we had just withdrawn from the bank was gone. Lesson learned: never let a crowd of people gather around you. Have them all move away from you as you speak to one person at a time. If they don't listen, then don't talk to anyone.

The Other Side of Slavery

The other side of the way some Ghanaians feel about slavery is how some show disdain for people who have a history of slavery in their family line. I've heard it mentioned among some Fante where a family was looked down upon because of having a history of servitude in their past. Even we have heard the word murmured "slave" derogatorily about us.

Many times Kofi felt in his dealings with some people that they held a superior attitude and spoke to him in a demeaning manner. He would tell them he didn't come to Ghana too trade one form of subjugation for another. This has only happen only two or three times but interesting enough to mention.

The Owner Will Show Up

When we had the boutique in town and people would stop in to window shop but not buy anything, they would just say, 'oh don't worry the owners of the merchandise will show up. If it takes a thousand years, the owners will show up." Meaning customers will certainly come to buy these items one day.

I'm Coming
It is typical when you are with a Ghanaian and they have to walk away, they will say "I'm coming" when actually they are leaving. They are going to come.

Stop Crying *He's Not Dead*
We met a man named *He's not dead*. Kofi and I wanted to know the story behind his name. He went on to tell us that one day when he was an infant as he appeared not to be breathing; everyone was alarmed and crying and screaming when his grandmother took him in a room and worked on him. A few minutes later she came out and said "stop crying, *he's not dead.*"

*

There are many other names used in Ghana that we never use on the other side for instance: *Innocent, Favor, Beautiful, Lovely, Bright, Holy, Perfect, Bible, Prosper, Think of me, Divine, Immaculate, Blessing, Wisdom, Fortune, Born Great, Gods Son, Cosmos and Treasure* to name a few. These names are usually used by Ewes from the Volta Region.

Store Names and Taxi and Tro-Tro Sayings
All the commercial taxis and *tro-tros* (an inexpensive passenger van) have all types of logos written on them. *Tro-tro* originally meant the cost of the fare was three pence. Going around Ghana one would think that this is surely a holy and righteous nation of people. The various religious themes are inspirational and some are amusing. Here is a list of a few of them: *Sweet Jesus Hair Salon, Don't Mind Your Wife Chop Bar, I Depend on God Alone Fashions, Because He Lives Tailoring, Are You God? Provisions, The Lord Cares Electricals, God Will See You through Phones, Who is free? Provisions* and there are thousands more.

*

There was a movie in America called Throw Mama from the Train. I call this story "Throw Mama from the Tro-Tro." This has happened to me three different times. I was sitting in the van minding my business and not listening to the discussion going on between the passengers and all of a sudden the driver and his mate said mama get down, mama get down and get a taxi to continue your journey.

They were changing their route to go a different way from the way they were initially headed; or at times I'm on a car that's headed to Accra but they want me to get down halfway and take a Cape Coast car because that's where I'm headed. Then they wanted me to pay them and I refused. Why should I pay you to throw me off the tro-tro? They don't linger to argue because they're always in a rush.

Caskets

A carpenter in Kaneshie, Accra has become famous since the 1960's by making creative hand carved caskets. Presently these casket making shops are opening around the country specializing in the one-of-a kind unique coffins. Each one can be made to correlate with the way the deceased lived their life or show the interests the person had. For instance a fisherman can have a large fish shaped coffin. A farmer could be buried in a large ear of corn coffin. I've seen a Star bottle of beer coffin. I guess this may have been their favorite drink.

The artisans are getting very creative and if the deceased was a mason a tool could be made into a coffin; or a painter etc. I didn't see it with my own eye but I've been told by Ann that she went to an auto mechanics funeral and he was somehow propped up in front of a car as if still working for the viewing of the body.

*

Someone else related at a teacher's funeral she was stunned to walk in and see the deceased propped up sitting at a desk. My friend Gisela had me admiring her bookcase of beautiful redwood. She then told me when she passes away it will be used as her casket for cremation by removing the shelves. What a way to get as much use from an item as you possibly can.

Still Learning

Watching people here carry things on their head is still so amazing to me. I remember my mother making us walk with books on our head; she said to promote good posture. However here in Ghana you'll see a person carry a refrigerator on their head, stacks of eggs, oranges, tomatoes, firewood, all sorts of things and rarely trip or fall along the crowded streets.

They will rather carry the smallest item on their head than in their hands. Some when they hear music will even cut a dance step and carry on with their stride. I've heard they can carry one third of their body weight on their heads. I still watch in amazement.

*

The folks who go around selling their wares on their heads I hear can walk almost forty miles a day to make their sales.

*

I like when people work in groups they sing in order to make the load lighter. When carpenters work they have a rhythm to how they hit their hammer. Auto mechanics have their radios and sing while they work. When Fishermen are pulling their nets in, they have a chant. Music is all around.

*

It's not uncommon to see a herd of cows and bulls walking the streets tying up traffic with their herdsmen taking them to find a place to graze. They just mosey along while you patiently or impatiently allow them to pass by.

*

When you ride a taxi you never know what a person may have with them when they join you. Someone could get in carrying live chickens, a goat. I even once I heard all this noise and saw people taking the biggest hog I've ever seen out of the boot (trunk) of a taxi. Getting ready for the "Pork Show" I guess. I've seen this sign outside a chop bar that sells light soup with pork.

*

I've seen many people over here who strikingly resemble people on the other side. I have literally seen people here I thought I knew from America.

Some people who look just like friends and relatives of mine. I thought I'd seen Queen, Artrice, Ruth, Carson, Newton, Diane, Alfred, Renee, Latif, Nia, Jabali, Dom, Tameka and Sylvia to name a few. I have even seen Tupac look-alikes and Bernie Mack (May their souls rest in perfect peace.)

*

I have been mistakenly thought to be a Ghanaian person someone knew. A gentleman came and joined me at the table in the restaurant where I was eating and greeted me. I was able to respond in Fante but then he rattled off in conversation and I had to respond that I speak English. He asked me, how are the children? I had to say that I'm sure he was thinking that I was someone else. He was astonished and thought I was someone named Nana he knew.

This has happened to me several times. Another time a gentleman approached me and asked me, how are the children? I replied there must be some mistake. He thought I was a police woman he knew. I love it!

*

We were never interested in football (soccer) in America. However when Ghana's teams are playing it is easy to catch soccer fever. The excitement is contagious, there is camaraderie in the air, everyone is happy and you can't help but want Ghana to win whomever they're playing.

We watched every game when Ghana's team played and even at times watched the UEFA league games which have Ghanaians on their teams. We wore Ghana's colors and waved Ghana's flag, we jubilated with every goal and game they won and lamented every lost game.

*

I overheard a conversation when someone was reprimanded for littering in the streets. The one who littered said if he didn't throw rubbish on the ground the street sweeper would have no job.

Wow! *"Ghana logic"* This is a phrase coined by a popular comedian here called KSM whom we love.

*

Cape Coast has their annual Fetu Afahye Festival every first Saturday of September. All the years we've been here we loved seeing it again and again. To see the exhibition of the expensive, colorful Kente cloth worn by chiefs and queens carried in their palanquins, the display of royal culture and tradition, the stool carriers, horn blowers, stilt walkers, and all the dancing and parading is a beautiful sight and reminder of our majestic past. It is a time when family comes together and many come home who reside outside the country. It is a weekend of parties and fun and the one time in a year the guesthouse is full.

*

I remembered our first Christmas here in Ghana, how I was so disappointed to see the nativity scenes with faces that didn't look Afrikan and also pictures of the Christ. I truly expected to come to Afrika and see religious symbolism in my own image. I didn't think it unreasonable.

I will certainly not dwell on this too much. In the first place the Bible says in Ex. 20:4KJV that "Thou shall not make unto thee any graven image, or any likeness of anything that is in heaven above." This makes me believe there shouldn't be any pictures or statutes at all.

However if you are going to use religious symbols let them reflect your own uniqueness since God made man in His image. Whoever you are He should look like you. Every other culture does appropriately to suit them.

Rev.1:13-15 KJV describes "One like unto the Son of man, his head and his hairs were like white wool; and his feet like unto fine brass; as if they burned in a furnace". Even the Black Madonna is worshipped in various churches in Europe. Hello. Is anyone listening?

*

I wonder with all the sunshine here on the continent of Afrika, why we are not the leaders in the solar energy industry. Our scientists and engineers are more than capable. Is there no interest?

*

There is a myth believed by most Ghanaians that all the foreigners who come here are rich. It is true our money may stretch further in this economy. We also run out of money too. While driving around Elmina town crossing the bridge at the fishing harbor many guys would holler and call out "Kofi God, Kofi God." He asked them why do you call me that, don't call me God? They responded, "Oh but you've got the dollars man."

*

The small one room kiosks may have a multiplicity of services available to you. One I saw advertised haircut, paint, passport pictures, nsu (water), phone cards, phone service, sharpening school students' pencils and charging of cell phones, all offered in one small room. The name of the store is *No Bribe at Heaven's Gate*. Smart man, see a need and fill it, business makes the world go round.

*

Whenever we went to church we were treated as if we were celebrities. We'd be asked to sit on the dais and start off the offerings. We were often asked to functions and made to chair programs, and given multiple donation envelopes because of the money we would bring in. We tired of this. the pretense was too obvious and we began visiting different congregations but haven't joined a specific church.

*

Did you ever think that funerals could be the source of social life? Well in Ghana it certainly is. There are funerals every weekend. The affair goes on for three days and the costs are very high and many families go into debt. It is a time of tears and grief for the family and chief mourners. However for the multitude it's a time of fashion, style and after the burial, merry making begins with the biggest boom box speakers ever seen.

The DJ is spinning the latest tunes, the feasting and party begins. Many folks will show up just for the food and drink and may not know the deceased well. Maybe they've only seen the person around and know of them. It is felt the grander the funeral the happier you make the deceased.

*

When you visit Ghana you will no doubt shop at the cultural center in Accra. It can be an overwhelming experience. The artisans and sellers seem very desperate to have you buy their wares. Some will adorn you with the jewelry and clothing they sell as you walk by. All sorts of marketing strategies are tried in order to get the money out of your pocket.

Learn the money equivalents, be friendly but firm and negotiate your price. Have a last price limit that you won't exceed to pay for an item. Never take the first price offered. You are considered very foolish if you don't attempt to bargain a bit. It is still frustrating for me to bargain coming from the other side where there's a sales price tag for everything.

I never know what the real cost of an item is or what is a fair price for services and repairs. Note that foreigners pay two to three times more than what a native will pay for the same item.

*

I recommend if you are coming and going back and forth from the states to Ghana that you find a couple of young children to sponsor their education throughout their elementary, junior and senior high school levels and even farther if you have the financial means. This way prayerfully you will nurture those who'll feel beholden to you enough to be forthright with you.

I've seen this work well with my neighbor Kojo Bey who cared for a young boy named Kofi since he was ten years old. The two of them have as close a relationship as father and son now. Kojo sponsored Kofi from elementary school to computer school after his senior high graduation. Kofi is respectful and honest with Kojo and protective of him when it comes to transactions with others. Maybe it's Kofi's good character or maybe it's due to the long standing relationship that their bond is so secure.

*

Everything is money matter here in Ghana. "Two man talk." You can get mostly anything, buy your way out of any trouble, or have any service done if only you have the money. Not much seems to be done out of friendship. Even work done for some churches by the members, they all want to be paid I'm told.

At times a person may want to donate a library or community center to a village and they ask for the labor to be provided freely as they provide the materials to build. This is not acceptable in most cases. The people want to be paid. I can speak of one Afrikan sister Cynthia Dillard from America who managed to have the cooperation of some members of her chosen village to build a community center freely as she gave them the supplies to build. At times I feel money is God here. Then on occasion when I reach in my pocket to pay someone for a good deed they'll back away and refuse to accept the money. These times are truly like breaths of fresh air.

*

We love Ghana music *pa pa pa!* (Very much) Ever since we touched down in Ghana we loved the beat and the singing of the music here. The first music we purchased was of Daddy Lumba, Papa Yankson, Osibesa, Kojo Antwi, Esther, and Daughters of glorious Jesus, to name a few. We like the old time high life better but some of the new hip life is okay if they don't copy the west too much and all the gospel music is good but we're partial to the uplifting praise music than the mournful sorrowful tunes.

*

We are happy to report that at times young people have come to us for employment and if we had no position for them, we would refer them to another establishment where they were hired and are still doing well. Our friends Sonia and Byron of Almond Tree Hotel are happy that we saw the potential in one such person named Anna we sent their way whom they've taken on board. Sometimes you can see the light in a person's eyes, good appearance, listen to their speech and know that they sincerely want a better life and are willing to work for it. There should be employment for such people. It is too disheartening to tell good people there's no vacancy.

However the fact is we have been subsidizing our business in order to remain open since its inception and if we didn't go in our own pocket the business would go under. So we can no longer keep hiring people if our budget does not allow nor if the customer patronage is not enough to cover the expenses. We simply look at the situation as our charity work until such time it improves. We are doing all we can through our monthly allotment here and grateful to God for all we can do.

*

We like to give many donations anonymously rather to have God reward us than men. As a teenager I loved the television program called the Millionaire when a man would show up at someone's door to give a million dollars from his employer who wanted to remain anonymous. My friends always said they wished he'd knock at their door and give them a million dollars but I said no; I wanted to be the person able to give out the millions of dollars. In Ghana our small pension allows us to be millionaires when the dollars are converted to cedis.

Ghanaian Food

We've planted a garden and grow foods so we can make our own salads. Moses planted lettuce, carrots, green pepper, cucumber, and cabbage; we also have, palm nut, paw-paw trees (papaya), coconut tree, sweet apple, lemon tree, avocado tree, banana trees and plantain trees.

I use the nim (neem) tree leaf powder as our pesticide. After being in Ghana a while I began to start buying the foods sold by traders on the street. I'd see different foods I was curious about and sampled them. I quickly learned my lesson. I wound up having stomach pains, diarrhea, vomiting and visiting the doctor for antibiotics. I learned I can't eat off the street perhaps due to the hygiene practices that were not safe in the preparation of the food; or perhaps the water used was not of good quality. I have to restrict myself to only eating in restaurants or in the homes of people I know personally.

The only food I can still eat from the street vender is the roasted plantain and the groundnuts or peanuts. I assume this is because it's hot off the grill. Now there is not much Ghanaian food that I don't like. I enjoy kenkey and fish with pepper, banku, fish and pepper, light soup, groundnut soup, omo tuo, palaver sauce, red-red, pusna, goat, lamb, chicken, lobster, prawns, cassava, yam, fried rice, jollof rice and nkontonmeri, all so good. (*Eye de oo*) This means so delicious.

Language

Everyone wants to know how we managed with the language. I was more conscientious to learn when we first arrived. I'd write words down in a book the way they sounded to me. I desired to learn a word a day. I bought books on speaking Fante but found it difficult to pronounce the words without hearing them.

I've learned enough greetings to make Ghanaians astonished and happy that I've tried to speak it. However it seems I've just been away too long and cannot even fix my tongue and mouth in the way a Ghanaian can. There's seventy-five various dialects across the country and even some Ghanaians need interpreters when they travel outside their residential zones.

There are so many nuances and intonations I can't even hear the differences between words and they sound the same. Even when I think I'm saying a word proper it's not heard the same when I speak it so I'm not understood. Someone may teach you words and you don't realize it may be a Ga word or Twi and you wind up speaking it to a Fante and it can all get really confusing. Although in the Akan language people who speak it can hear the similarity between words. I know how to ask for the price of my purchase to be reduced: *te me su ka kra*, and that's very important to me.

*

I love it when a Ghanaian comes up to me speaking the native language assuming I understand because they think by my physical appearance that I should be able to respond to them in Fante. I love that. It means to me that I look like I belong here-as long as I don't open my mouth. When I speak, I remove all doubt.

Yet since most people here speak English it's not a big problem communicating except you do have to be sure you and the person are on the same page. I've sent for bread and the person returned with a blade (razor blade) and asked ice and received rice so make sure that you are understood. I've asked for cocoa and received corn dough.

Too many times I hear "Oh I thought you said this or I thought you said that.

I don't understand your intonation is said to me frequently.

Although there are times you may come across a laborer who is good at their craft but did not attend school and doesn't speak any English then you have to work through an interpreter.

*

I love my life here in Ghana. I love Ghanaian's; most I've met are very friendly, they have lovely smiles and personalities, happy carefree attitudes, jovial, helpful, forgiving, patient, resourceful, beautiful and proud people. They don't take themselves so seriously and can laugh at themselves. There was a worldwide poll taken on which countries have the happiest people and Ghana placed eighth in the world. Ghanaians have a reputation for being hospitable.

I like the differences between Ghana and America which are almost two extremes. I like Ghana because of the differences; but I see the gap lessening in some ways due to the western influence on Ghanaian society. Since coming in 1999 I see western influence in dress and hair styles for men and women, music, dance, philosophy whereas the grass seems greener, the water seems wetter, and the sugar is sweeter it's felt outside of Ghana.

At times it appears respect for Ghanaian Tradition and respect for elders is decreasing. Too much outside influence on the television is changing values here and not all for the better. Courtesy towards women and the elderly especially on public transportation is dying. A man will push a woman aside to take a seat on public transportation. The newspapers say that drug activity is increasing here. I was watching a Ghanaian beauty pageant but when a singer with his pants half down exposing his underwear came on stage I turned the television off. I don't want to see Ghana pick up some of the same negative characteristics that are dragging down the USA.

God bless our homeland Ghana, and make our nation great and strong.
Bold to defend forever, the course of freedom and of right.
Fill our hearts with true humility. Make us cherish fearless honesty.
And help us to resist oppressors rule with all our will and might forever more.

These are the words to Ghana's National Anthem and *everyone* living in this country should take them to heart because they are true words to live by.

Be Black, Shine, Aim High
Leontyne Price

Where Is The Authentic Afrikan?

We were shocked to come here only to find so many sisters bleaching their skin, not seeming to love the beautiful black skin they're in and not very "happy to be nappy". There are not many women wearing natural hair styles. Too many men and women here choose western clothes over their own beautiful traditional outfits. Too many have adopted foreign names. Public servants had to be forced to at least wear traditional clothing on Fridays to work.

On the other side I had the notion that I'd meet nationalistic Afrikans once arriving here. I figured the original "I'm black and I'm proud" folks would greet me and welcome me home. Contrarily many Continental Afrikans want to trade places with us or any other westerner.

All of us who have lived where we were dominated by foreigners will find we have too much of the "other" mind in us from their colonial ruling. I see many vestiges of British rule still evident. One change I would make would be the blond colonial wigs worn by lawyers and judges in the courtrooms. I'll donate some black afro wigs if they'd accept them. . Likewise after coming here I have to admit I'm more Americanized than I am Afrikan. I don't know if we can ever fully de-program ourselves?

I believe I'll have to visit Ethiopia to find the true Afrikan. I believe it's one of the few Afrikan countries not colonized for a long period by foreign invaders. I plan to visit Ethiopia one day and hope to find Afrikans who truly love themselves and are proud of their culture, not wanting to be anyone else but who they are.

There have been many a Ghanaian we've talked to who have stated those of us in the Diaspora was blessed by slavery. Many persons with this warped view were intellectuals and in vocations of banking and teaching. More than a couple of Ghanaians have asked us how we could ever leave America to come to live in Ghana.

They could not perceive such a decision and remarked that if a ship were docked with a sign on it saying slaves wanted they'd be the first one aboard. I forgive them because they don't know the ramifications of what they are saying.

We in the Diaspora were blessed in *spite* of slavery. I feel that most Ghanaians cannot empathize with us from outside regarding what an emotional subject it is for us who have been affected by the slave trade. I've even been told jokingly to "get over it." How hard it seems for many of them to walk in our shoes. No I didn't personally experience it but feel the burden of it, the horrors of it just as if I were on the slave ship and in the cotton fields.

There's a big difference in the colonialism experienced by Ghanaians in their own country by their exploiters, the Portuguese, British, French, Dutch, Swedish, Danish, and the colonialism Afrikans in America endured.

There was also slavery in early traditional Ghana although properly named a caste system. However their method rewarded "slaves" who served well by including them as members of the household and over the years were allowed to own property and even given their freedom at a certain point in time.

Truly Ghanaians probably cannot relate at all to our experience; because their plight although brutish may have been moderate by our comparison. The treatment in transit to the America's and once on land was abominable and inhuman for our ancestors. Animals were treated better.

There is no similarity. How can Ghanaians understand us on this level? Afrikan American history is not readily taught in the public school system here either. Many of them laugh when we tell our stories and don't even show a compassionate humanity. I guess the conversation just makes them too uncomfortable to face. Most Ghanaians have not visited the slave dungeons. There is a gulf between us in this area. Although the public school system is beginning to send their children to visit the slave dungeons to learn of the history. We all have to look in the mirror to decide how we will play our own part to restore sanity to our people and our Mother Afrika.

"Few things can help an individual more
Than to place responsibility on him and
To let him know that you trust him"
Booker T. Washington
(Or her-emphasis mine)

Thin Line Between Family And Friend

Where does the line between acquaintance, friend and family end and begin? There are some friends that are closer than family members. At times there are family members you'd never choose as friends. In Ghana some people I would call acquaintance would say we are friends.

I love it the way the term cousin is not used here. In Ghana your cousins are called your sisters and brothers and your uncle is called father and your aunties are your mothers. There's no estrangement, no separation, family is one. Something all of humanity has to learn, we are all one.

My good friends Lee J. and Netfa whom I told you I met by the Spirit and not by coincidence, but by a divine appointment. I think you can now see how beautifully the Creator set this up. They are also angels sent along our pathway.

Although Kofi and I had decided to come to Ghana, I can bet you if we had not met angel Anastasia Hooper through them; we'd have a whole different story to tell. If I had not obeyed the voice of Spirit to speak to Lee J. there is no telling our fate alone as strangers in Accra.

The Harold's came to our going away party before we left the States and kept in touch by phone almost weekly. When they came over for Lee

J's first visit to Ghana, we enjoyed ourselves too much! Lee J. can keep us all laughing and he's a good singer. He even made his debut at Fairhill Guesthouse with a song he made up on the spot called "Come to Cape Coast."

In their suitcase they brought a care package of many items we missed from the other side like Tastycakes, pancake mix, syrup, grits, salmon, clams, Long Island Iced Tea and the list goes on. These two are as close to us as family, even closer. They've shown their love in many ways and walk the talk. Kofi and I found them dependable enough to count on for anything that we asked. We would do the same for them.

We always had fun together and never had a cross word until one day for no apparent reason a jealous streak rose up in Kofi against Lee J. concerning me. He refused to talk to them over the phone for a few months. Then later as mysteriously as this sudden behavior came it left and Kofi was calling him 'my son" again.

All was well again in our friendship but Lee J. and Netfa said it hurt them and made them feel like orphans during that estranged time. All I could do was pray. I am so glad this was settled before Kofi made his transition.

I can truly say that Lee J. and Netfa, the Abanyie clan, and my friends of Afrikan Diasporas here became our extended family. My blood sisters, nieces and nephews, and many friends on the other side seemed to have forgotten about us.

No one on the other side seemed inquisitive about Afrika or about how we were getting along, although some of them did remember my birthday and sent me a text message during the year.

I guess this is part of the sacrifice of going out to follow your truth, giving up one thing to take on something else. I shrugged it off as everyone being caught up in the rat race over there. It seemed we were just out of sight and out of mind. Although I felt the distance was no excuse for us not to stay in communication in this day of text messages, e-mails and Skype. I did my part to keep in touch.

However family is family and just like our two eyes never see each other but they are there for each other; my family has an invisible thread that connects our hearts and distance can't erase it as far as I'm concerned. Now that my nieces and nephews are growing up they're now reaching out to me over the internet on their own which makes me very happy. I'm hoping some will want to visit soon.

What's so amazing was my son's visit with my best friends Lee J. and Netfa. I acquired a three month bank loan to expedite purchasing cement, sand, tiles, paint, furniture, electrical supplies, linens and all I needed to meet my deadline to finish the guest rooms at Promise Land for their arrival. When October 4th, 2009 came I was the happiest mother in the world at Kotoka Airport to greet my son Latif (Tee) and my good friends. Another desire fulfilled! What a longing that has come to pass. What a miracle my Lord!

Hope deferred can make the heart sick. I have been in Ghana going on ten years and this is the first visit from a family member. I thought I'd not celebrate my birthday since Kofi has left me but now I have a reason to celebrate because my son will be in Ghana on my birthday! What an *akwaaba* (welcome) party it will be.

The cultural group was assembled, friends were seated but I wouldn't start the program until Sister Ann arrived who was busy on one of her many "angel" missions causing her delay. She was busy helping someone somewhere. Once she arrived the processional started with Aunt Leticia's female horn blowers in front announcing the special occasion.

Aunties' School of Afrikan Rhythm and Dance drummers followed the special guests while young ladies threw flower petals for my son and friends to walk upon as they were guided to their seats at the high table. (Does this sound familiar from a movie?) The look on my sons face was priceless, his mind was blown and he was definitely overwhelmed being the focus of attention.

The gathering stood and clapped as they entered. I exclaimed to everyone how elated I was to introduce my son to them and proceeded to have him stand to be wrapped in our traditional family cloth by our Chief Nana Afrakoh who sat him on the stool and gave him his Fante name Ekow for being born on Thursday.

Talcum powder was showered over him and the song Welcome Home was played for him and my friends now named Kojo (Monday born) and Ama (Saturday born). We had a good time, there was dancing, birthday cake for me, Kojo presented a lovely photograph to Ann, and Imakus sang a beautiful song 'Thank You Lord' to round up the day's activities.

The stool is an important symbol in Ghanaian culture. It is a symbol of unity between the ancestral world and the living members of the clan. It is a special gift to be given on many important occasions and signifies power and unity. It is equivalent to a throne.

My son thoroughly enjoyed his three week stay in Ghana. I was happy because I admit Ghana is not for everyone. You either adapt or you leave. Latif said he'd like to be here six months and help me but also live in the USA six months to make money to return here.

Yes, that would be a perfect life for some folks who are not yet retired but have the flexibility with their career to do this. Since he's in barber school, as a barber he could manage going and coming. He must have received a hundreds hugs, handshakes and akawaaba's from everyone I boasted to "meet my son Ekow."

The adventurer he is he even traveled by tro-tro to find the Sunday Market to shop for clothes. Ask him about the food and he'll tell you he never ate such fresh fish and lobster in his life and the pineapples are the sweetest he's ever tasted. Latif said to me "who are you? I don't even know you anymore. You're over here living like a queen, while I'm over there struggling". He shook his head in disbelief.

He could hardly believe his legacy, the guesthouse and the house on the hill with the ocean view is exquisite. He will certainly return. This legacy is here for anyone in the Merritt Clan to come and enjoy temporarily or permanently.

My Abanyie family will oversee the property in my absence until any of my family members on the other side realize they have a choice besides the USA to live.

The Abanyie family can manage the properties, live in the properties, until my family in America wakes up to their inheritance that is waiting here for them. I want the property to be here time immemorial and whosoever will come, let them come. If they don't come let my Abanyie family, manage it and enjoy it. I never want it sold. Kofi's and I soul and spirit are on these lands. It's a spiritual thing, many won't understand and it's not to be capitalized upon but revered.

When I visited family stateside in 2006, Kofi didn't want to come saying he'd never take his feet off Afrikas' soil once they were planted here. After Kofi passed I visited in July of 2010 for a family reunion, because the family hadn't come together since my first trip four years earlier.

They went all out for my arrival and the television show Soul Food's spread had no contest with ours and we enjoyed ourselves. All my nieces and nephews have grown so and some who were not even born when we left in 1999 are: Sincere, Sidero, Jaylyn, Amayah, and Khamia, and Troy Jr. just an infant when we left.

I'd like to get together with them biannually but I also desire for them to visit Ghana before I make my transition. Sometimes we want things for people that they don't want for themselves. My greatest wish is to have them come altogether as a group. If I had the finances I would have arranged it by now.

During that visit I also reunited with old co-worker and friend Joyce S., also with friends I hadn't seen for thirty years Diane C., and Olympia R. When you are friends for so long aren't you just like family?

"When I fight about what is going on in the neighborhood,
Or when I fight about what is happening to other peoples
Children, I'm doing that because I want to leave a community
And a world that is better than the one I found"
Marian Wright Edelman

We Are Family

We have a family that is growing in our area of the Central Region. There is a concentration of those from our tribe of Afrikan Americans in the Central Region.

We are all here building bridges in many ways. Some of us have businesses, non-governmental organizations or NGO's, some just one on one in our daily interactions promote cultural exchange and solidify relationships with our new family of Ghanaian brothers and sisters.

Good Examples
Moses
Kofi and I told all our employees that we were willing to assist them to buy a plot of land in our town and help them build a structure on it for them to live in. The only condition was for them to work with us for two years before we would start the process and we hoped they would work with us for a minimum of two years or more after completion of the project.

One day our grounds-keeper Moses asked if he could sleepover at our place because his sister-in-law was visiting and she would sleep in the bed with his wife. He was renting a room in the town and we asked him why didn't he buy a plot of land and build a house on it. He lowered his head and replied he could never do that.

We wondered why he would think that way and told him that he could buy land because he was working and making a salary. So we showed him how he should go to the chief of the town and ask him to show him plots for sale and inquire the cost. We told him we'd save a portion of his pay towards the purchase of the plot.

However he got so excited after speaking with the chief and found a plot of land he liked that he asked us to loan him the GHC150.00 at the time for the plot and take partial deductions from his pay monthly. It was the Nana who didn't want to accept partial payments and wanted the lump sum.

Moses purchased some mud blocks and we bought some cement for him; and he built a three room house for his wife and three children. He has thanked us so many times for helping him dream something he never dared to dream for himself. He's even expanding and adding more rooms to his home and rebuilding it himself.

Moses is a very smart young man and a fast learner. He left our employment for a couple of years to learn carpentry and when he returned he became even more valuable to our establishment. He is really like a son to us. He is the only Ghanaian who has taken us up on our offer to work with us towards a long term goal. His peers in the village used to laugh at him calling him *garden boy* but now he is envied and mentoring another young man named Ben.

We know there are others out there somewhere but so many have turned us down. Most have said they want to live in the city and not on the outskirts where we're located as their reason for refusing our offer. We would like to duplicate this project with other persons. We found that a part of the poverty here is a poverty of the mind. There's a poverty of ideas and dreams, along with a feeling of hopelessness and dependency. Some are dependent upon others always giving to them, yet many work laboriously from sunup to sundown.

Elizabeth

As Kofi and I sat on the summer hut chilling one morning, an older woman approached with a young girl begging us to give the girl just out of JSS (junior secondary school) a job. *Maame* introduced her daughter to us as Elizabeth. She had no skills or training to work at the hotel but neither Kofi nor I liked turning people away who came looking for work if we could help it. We asked Elizabeth if she really wanted to work and she said that she did. So we told her to come and assist Mr. Menser the elderly man who did our washing and ironing and learn from him and we'd give her a small allotment for coming twice a week. She did so well that when Mr. Menser retired she was able to take over his job.

After a while we started letting Elizabeth train as a housekeeper for the motel rooms and she excelled at this too. After being with us for a couple of years she told of her desire to go back to school for catering at a vocational school in another town and we wished her well.

However the next year we found her home frequently and inquired only to find out that the family ran out of funds and she stopped her program. They never came to us for help but we decided to take on the responsibility of financing the rest of her education for the next three to four years. She'd work for us during her holiday time off from school and on the Saturdays of her weekends as she continued to excel at learning all areas of hotel work.

She even learned to greet the customers, register guests, serve customers, shop, and assist the cooks in the kitchen. We could see her growth and the confidence she was building in herself. This past week she had her cooking exams at school and feels she did well as she has one more year of study. We are so proud of her and will be happy to hire her as a full time cook in the future.

These are the kinds of things Kofi and I wanted to do on a larger scale but sorrowfully many people pass through our gates but don't have long term goals. Many of the folks we meet don't even dare to dream. Some of the folks make enough money for the month and they're off to who knows where. They don't even say goodbye. It's like we have a revolving door of people coming and going, appearing sincere at the onset and talking as if they intend to be with us always.

There is a lack of hope and no desire to stick around for any goal planning. We've paid for several other students tuition with no strings attached and they've gone on to greener pastures which is great! Some were appreciative and some were ungrateful. Some have repaid our good deeds with contempt. There are all kinds of people in the world no matter where you are in the world and we always reap what we sow wherever we are.

Central Region of Ghana

We are all here with Afrika on our minds and Afrika in our hearts participating in the reuniting of the Afrikan family. Aunt Fannie Clarke an octogenarian at eighty-six years is our eldest mother in the community who keeps us in awe with her wit and agility. She is frequently teaching Ghanaians in her community math and reading skills in her home. Jintz her niece is my soul sister in Teshie who has an awesome legacy to bring forth-a birthing clinic and mid wife facility left to her by her mother Mrs. Lola.

Dr. Nana Ama E. Malkia Brantuo is the Queen Matriarch of our Family and keeps trying to have us come together to work on a group project other than partying. Getting together for a party can be done at the drop of a hat, monies can be contributed, venues organized and before you know it we're on the floor *"stepping for love.* However Mame Malkia has formed a group of palm tree growers and spearheaded the forming of a credit union.

Mable's Table owners Rabbi Halevi and Mable are the spiritual leaders of the Bereshith Hebrew Israelites. Rabbi Kohain is also the Executive Secretary of Panafest Foundation and a walking history book. I always leave his presence having learned something new. Mable has the gift of hospitality catering for large groups of people. I love their children Kwame and Awushi as my own. Dear Elder Amram, Kohains' father has made his transition to join the ancestors. Peace!

Mr. and Mrs. Ed and Bertha Brown are the most adorable married couple of elders we have. Bert has a do-it-herself home remodeling spirit and Ed is teaching folks to make wine and he is another one of our resident historians.

One Africa's Wellness Resort Owner Imakus is a shiny star in her own right, has brought Chi Gong exercising to us and I was so happy to learn. She has helped villages get bore holes for water, medical attention for needy individuals and she has learned to be a mid wife while living in Ghana. Shabazz the entertainer is always keeping a smile on our faces, urging us to become vegetarians, and has bridged the cultural divide through marriage into Ghanaian families which has brought forth two beautiful children. Sorrowfully Nana Ben has left us to be an ancestor. Rest peacefully.

Sar Rueben and wife Sarah have a home worthy of House Beautiful Magazine. Brother Haseed and Sister Aisha are our musicians and singers extraordinaire. Sister Nkiruka with her shiny red motorcycle has also cut a music CD. Brother Israel has linked up with a Ghanaian hotelier and they all are building bridges one on one with people in their communities..

Prof. Yaa Asantewa and Nana Kweku have the look of Masai Tribe Royalty has legally adopted Ofosu and has him enrolled in Cape Polytechnic and prepared to assist him as far as he aspires to go in his education-even to graduate school.

My sister Sonia and brother Byron of Almond Tree Guesthouse are our Regae connection "yea mon." They have sponsored Saturday school, reading programs, and formed Soni-Bron an NGO to bring in large containers of donated books, furniture and other well needed items for schools in Elmina from London.

Sister Queen is behind the scenes in Eguafo, Elmina way in the hinterland helping empower women with micro loans to do petty trading. I thank her so much for standing in my stead during my stay on the other side.

Dr. Pat Leonard is another one of our scholars who worked extensively with the African Burial Ground Project in New York and had hopes of using her place here as a healing space.

Nana Prempeh who will always tell us to have a great Garvey day and his wife Nana Afia is Ghanaian and headmistress at a school in their community would show Black History videos to Ghanaians to teach them our story in America.

Dr. Nancy Fairley from Davidson College in N.C. has a student exchange program established at UCC. One of her Ghanaian students Kojo has implemented an afterschool program in Kwapro teaching reading, math and French to approximately eighty students. He has volunteers who assist him and Nancy achieved a real "each one teach one" model through his efforts.

We have the founder of Sabayet community in Dutch Komenda Nana Kofi who will be bringing others to join us through his housing project and he has employed a number of top notch artisans. Brother John Parker who's wife Harrett passed away a month before my Kofi (their Fante names also Kofi and Adjoa) is with us seeking to cherish her memory as he moves on to the next chapter in his life is establishing an educational scholarship program for Ghanaian students. Mother Gerri is sensitive to our Ancestral Spirits. Her son Power and his wife Future are artists who've made a music video called Holla Blak.

Brother Kojo Bey and his father Abeshi are my neighbors who are drumming artists and are busy helping orphaned children through their NGO. They rescue children who have been taken from their families to work with fishermen. At times families let the children go to work because they need the money. They find ways to help the families obtain an alternate income and return the children home.

Mwenda and Japhiyah and their children wanted to create a butterfly sanctuary. Amiciah and his Ghanaian wife Naomi are building their own community in Asin Foso with their six children now that recent twins are blessed to join their family. There's a group of Afrikans' from the other side to join them to develop a community complete with hospital, police station, school and synagogue.

Mama Kali started a group for grand-mothers interested in the future of our next generation of young folks, and introduced moringa tree farming. Dr. Roth to us who blessed me with some good old blues music I'm listening to as I write will engage in holistic medicine.

We have the Oiada Group family who lives in the purple house who sing the praises of Jehovah, Ben, Berkeyah and Noamyah are with the group of Isrealites who run Asasse Pa Health Resort in Cape Coast keeping us fit through various healing modalities.

Bro. Daveed and Malka engage in organic farming in Kasoa, along with Bro. Kareem and his wife Sunkwa also keeping us healthy through farming in Cape Coast.

Dr. Angel is our Chiropractor will soon marry a Ghanaian celebrity P.Y. Mr. and Mrs. Jeff and Shikera Edison are building their ocean front home in Elmina and working towards the day when they can spend more time in Ghana.

Haqikah Salim produces soap and her mom Mrs. Shirley McCall are in Kasoa, Kalisha has a radio program and works with the Office of Youth & Employment has married a Ghanaian named Ebow, we have adopted each other as family.

Prof. Tarin Hampton is teaching dance at the University of Cape Coast (UCC) and Prof. Howard Grisby also teaching at UCC in the Sociology Dept. are new to our area and welcome.

Sorrowfully our sister Alimiesha Jaliwa who was assisting the Hoteliers Association and other groups when she suddenly made her transition recently to join the ancestors, leaving her daughter Aziza and grandson Kweku. We organized her fortieth-day memorial and as a family-community of Diaspora and indigenous Afrikans' and gave her a final sendoff befitting the life she led as a community organizer here in Ghana. May she have eternal rest!

Central Region Association of Afrikan Ascendants in Ghana

This is the core of a family group that I'm sure will grow exponentially. We have many persons who come and go stateside but still belong to us and fit right in upon their return. I'm only counting persons in our immediate locale of the Central Region

Some of us formed ourselves into a group called (CRAAAG) the Central Region Association of Afrikan Ascendants in Ghana. No doubt we are the descendants of our ancestors who made that terrible Trans Atlantic trip to the Americas; but we are ascending towards our rightful destiny.

The ancestors tapped us on our shoulders and beckoned us to come home and we have heard and obeyed their call. We are all here ascending on a path towards our individual birthrights and a collective mission yet to be clearly defined. Something is spiritually stirring. I pray we have ears to hear what the Spirit is saying.

African American Association in Ghana

Many American Africans are here scattered all over the country, and some have come and gone back never to return again. There's a concentration of our clan in the Volta Region also. A few are here of which the only thing we have in common is that we are all here in Ghana together and nothing more. That's just the way it is. Also the African American Association in Ghana (AAAG) is a group based in Accra representing returning Africans from America and is open for membership. We have an Office of Diaspora Affairs led by Dr. Erika Bennett and a Coalition of various interest groups have come together to formally address pressing agenda matters we face as a total Afrikan family unit.

It is yet to be determined the financial impact we as a group are contributing directly towards Ghana's GNP but we're positive it is a substantial amount. It is definitely enough to afford us some clout and recognition to have our concerns heard and deliberated upon with sincerity by the powers that be.

Queen E. Malkia Brantuo

Sadly, 8th November, 2010, Bro. Ruben called me approximately 8:30pm and said "We've lost Big Mama." I felt as if an earthquake rumbled beneath my feet. I called her almost thirty times but the phone lines wouldn't connect throughout the day. Mama asked Sarah to call me and I asked her how did she feel today? "Well my stomach is paining me and my legs feel like water, other than that I'm okay" she said. This was a term I couldn't relate to at the time. Yet as soon as I heard the news of her passing away I related instantly. If a chair had not been near for me to sit on I would have spilled onto the floor, unstable just like water myself. Big Mama said the doctor gave her medication and we both said we'd see each other tomorrow. Tomorrow came but mama Malkia was gone.

She did not sound like death was lurking at her door. I would have been at her side at any hint of such a thing. Dr. Nana Maame, I called her frequently and it always made her laugh. I have leaned on you spiritually and emotionally for so long and did not realize just how much until this moment, now that you have vanished! I felt as though I've been walking with crutches and someone has snatched them from me and I'm going down fast.

Big Mama you were a class act, a one in a million. I have never met anyone like you who personified peace, love, joy, mercy, poise, patience, calm, generosity, royalty, inner and outer beauty, honesty, authenticity, strength, wisdom, grace, cooperation, unity, determination, vision, and Divinity. She was another Angel.

Rabbi Kohain and Mother Gerri gave us comforting words that night as the family all came together. Yes we will cry awhile, but we have to dry our eyes and endeavor to live on with Mama Malkia's life as an example of a life well lived. She was a pillar of strength for us all and we must follow her example. She named her beautiful oceanfront property Sankofa Sanctuary.

The Most High allowed Mama to leave the planet on her own terms. Although she didn't feel fine and the doctor visited her at home that day she was her normal cheerful self, apologizing for having to be tended to and not wanting to complain. She talked and laughed with family and when they left her side she gave up the ghost.

Big Mama knew how to make everyone feel special. She had the gift of charisma, was a beacon of light and love, and made an indelible mark on so many lives on two continents. I have lost a spiritual mother, a friend, and a confidant.

Our entire community of Ghanaians and Afrikan Americans committed themselves in solidarity from beginning to end to assist her daughter Chekesha grant all Big Mama's burial wishes. There were certain traditional rites to be performed because she was Queen of the village of Akotokyir, the cremation service, the celebration of life party and lastly the fortieth day ceremony with her ashes released into the Atlantic Ocean in front of her home as she wished. The hardest demand of hers to comply with was for us not to cry and lament over her transition.

Big Mama's school Akoma International Academy of Arts and Sciences serves children in one of the poorest villages Ayensudo in the central region and donations are needed to keep the school opened. We as a community will stand together with Mama Malkia's daughter Chekesha to keep this school viable in order to educate children who might not ever be educated due to poverty. It costs only $270.00 per year to pay for the education of one student and anyone who loves educating children please contact akomainternationalacademy.com.. Reach out and change a child's life forever. Marian Wright Edelman has said "The question is not whether we can afford to invest in every child it is whether we can afford not to." In Ghana to attend school itself is free but the miscellaneous and necessary items required such as books, uniforms, transportation, lunch, and all sorts of school fees are not free and too many families cannot afford it. Many would rather send their children out to hawk (work) selling petty items on the street or send them to the farm to meet their immediate needs. The rewards of education seem too far away especially to those in the rural areas.

Ghanaian extended Family

Ghanaians have also formed part of our family core: Dr. Andoh our Ethno-Botanist, Adjei, Jojo, Kojo, Sisco, Sam, The Quarshie family Uncle Ato, Lawrencia, Marcus and Eric, Tetteh, Adjo, Apombea, Nana Ifua, Maame Ifua, Becky, Doe and Lucy Grant, just to name a few. When we all get together socially or are bereaved they are among us as a part of our family.

I personally have Ghanaians who are close friends other than those in my Abanyie family and will name a few here and any folks who feel their name should have been here please charge the omission to my head and not my heart. There is Nana Afrakoh, Maame Pola, Maame Arthur, Kassim, Mr. Menser, Dellotte, Mallam Abuchie, Phillestina, Dr. Nat, Mr. Arhin, Dr. Cobbina, John Ekow Eshun, Mary Kweku, Regina Quacoe, Comfort, Odas Agustus, Mr. and Mrs. Agrey Fynn.

Mrs Aggie Boger and Peter, Joyce and Richard Mensah, Nana Ya, Gifty and Peter Saah, James Anquanda and Earsie who reminds me of my mother, Mrs. Mary Brown, Mrs. Sally Honsall, The Hoteliers Association of Central Region, Phillip-Mr. Esoteric, Mama Tee, Kofi Brookman, Perpetual, Mercy, Abraham and Marium, Hayfordsant and Fausti, Ras Tony, Alberto, Francis, Soloman and Mr. and Mrs. Frances and Kwesie Fynn and Black Star David of blessed memory. I mention these folks because they were all there for me when dear Kofi passed away; we have passed the associate stage to friendship. We've achieved something that was hoped would never materialize if some powers that be had their way.

You can read an article in the 2008 February edition of the New African Magazine that will explain efforts tried to prevent Afrikans from the Diaspora and Continental Afrikans from ever working together in unity. [3]

Read "Divide and rule." The movement towards a united Afrika will never die, but most assuredly the opposition against this cause will not cease either.

Golden Girls

I've made all kinds of friends here and frequently remark about all the loving people I would have never met if I had never come to Ghana. I meet monthly with two "golden girls", I admire how they age with grace. Both of these ladies can run circles around me, have so much energy, are intelligent and still learning; and I say when I grow up I want to be just like them.

Auntie Essie is Ghanaian and celebrated her eightieth birthday while Gisela is German and in her early seventies and I get pearls of wisdom from each of them.

---

[3] New Africa Magazine, February 2008, pages 72-75, Divide and rule...the report on 20, April 1978. Review Memorandum NSWC-46

All around the world

I enjoyed close friendship with Elicel from Cuba, and Gladys Eze from Cameroon. Then there are Marine miners, Ian, Bob, and Dale from Canada, Lothar from Germany and Yoki from Japan. Lucinda and her mother Yvonne from Surinam but live in Amsterdam still keep in touch and so many others.

Kukuwa and Papa Kofi

Most of the people who have worked with us are like family and one especially is Kukuwa (Joyce). I loved her like a daughter from the moment she came to us for employment. She didn't have any training in catering but was willing and a fast learner and was soon able to manage the site. She was with us a few years before she married Pastor Rhule and began to have children.

When she had her first boy she named him Papa Kofi after my husband. When she returned from her six month maternity leave we allowed her to bring the baby to work. He was so adorable and we took to him like a grandson so everyday 8am he was in our bed between Kofi and me. We blew bubbles, played with him, took pictures and videos of him since he was six months old.

This baby could hold Kofi's drum sticks and play the Djembe drum and fall asleep with the sticks still in his hands. He brought us so much joy! We celebrated his first Christmas with him and mommy. Kofi was so happy to go out and buy him all sorts of things: a crib, walker, outfits, bottles, blankets, toys, food, etc. We have copies of his hand and foot prints and marked the wall for his height so we can watch how he grows.

Papa was two years old when dear Kofi passed away. He didn't understand but could sense our sadness and we made an outfit for him to wear to the funeral. When he's older I'll show him the videos of him and his namesake. Now Kukuwa has a second child that we were hoping would be a girl to name Adjoa but God gave us another precious boy named Kweku. There's a swing and sliding board in the yard for them to play with.

Ann

Then there is my sister Ann whom the family says when her name is mentioned we should all stand and salute. She doesn't feel she is doing anything special. We call her our "Earth Angel". Kofi and I gave her a gold necklace with three hearts on it. We thought it signified her life as we saw it. Her life is shared out of her love for God, love for her family, and love for her community. I call her the Harriet Tubman of Ghana because she's helped so many relatives visit America to live and work.

Many say when you look up Ghana in the dictionary that Ann's picture should be there because she is truly a good ambassador for Ghana. I call her the unofficial mayor of Cape Coast because she is a mover and shaker and helps so many people.

She can add Repatriation Specialist to the list of her many talents; because she frequently assists Ghanaian friends and family living outside with their building plans so when they return home to Ghana their dwelling place is ready to move into.

We celebrated her sixtieth birthday this year where a crowd of family and friends from near and far showed their appreciation and gratitude to her for all her kindness. What a gala it was!

Abanyie Clan
Ann's parents Mr. Amos Abanyie and Mrs. Marion Bernice Steele-Dadzie Amos Abanyie had to be very special people to raise such a wonderful family. I hear that my big sister Aggie and Ann take after their mother the way they like to feed people and share with the less fortunate.

All of her brothers have big hearts and all of their wives are precious too. Other family members: Nana Gyan and wife Rebecca, Nicholas, Nathan, Natasha and Damon with their two little girls, Gabriel, Jacob, Sammy, the Haligah's, Auntie Aggie, FiFi, Roberta, Uncle Ebow, Rev.& Mrs. Asante, Rev. & Mrs. Ampiah, John and all my relatives in Tema, Shama and Takoradi along with so many others I cannot name here I love you all.

Ricky
My brother Ricky—Isaac Hooper, Ann's husband is a dead ringer for his cousin Hon. Kofi Anan former Secretary of the United Nations. I also had the pleasure of meeting him personally at their family house and even have a picture taken with him. He's very handsome in person, a quiet gentle giant, and very personable.

Sisters of the Ark

Spirit formulated a family as what happened with Sisters of the Ark; we all became very close in a short time. Twelve ladies were brought together in spirit for seven days of prayer to petition the Most High to move on behalf of the state of affairs concerning Afrika and Afrikans. Nana Adwoa was given the mandate, she and Dr. Zee marched carrying the ark in front and Onalie and I in the rear were entrusted with carrying many petitions that were written down and placed inside. The ark was finely crafted with angels on each end, painted gold and resembled the one described in Joshua chapter six in the Bible.

Zakia ushered the young maidens in front and blew the trumpets. Nana Zulu led us around the site once for six days and seven times the seventh day. When she poured libations and prayed her voice was liken to a wise primal priestess of olden days which caused me to travel back in time to ancient places, old landmarks and brought me to tears. Dr. Sharita was sent by the Spirit to fill in the gap on the last day. We were obedient to the command and are anxious to see the manifestation of God's hand ruling in favor of our people with a breakthrough in regards to a myriad of injustices we face as Afrikans'.

Since family can be defined in many ways I want to say family is found among people who show mutual respect and love and provide a nurturing bond of caring, sharing and concern for one another. Here in Ghana everyone is my brother or my sister, friends get merged into family and this family crosses bloodlines, is spiritual, physical, emotional, local and international. Family transcends all boundaries and defies separation. We are one family of humanity with one heart, one mind, one body, in one God. While most folks won't agree with me and many don't act as if this is true, it's true for me.

"Everything in your world is created by what you think."
Oprah Winfrey

On My Own

I am often asked am I not I lonely living in Ghana alone without my husband or any relatives here with me? Don't you secretly miss all the material things in the States? Although I do miss my family in the states and Kofi very much, I can truly say I am not lonely here. Kofi and I made a nice life here. Our properties have no mortgage on them. I have God-given friends and family surrounding me. I'm secure in Gods' love for me, I am never really alone.

Alone we come into the world and alone we leave. I can always find something to keep me occupied. Every time I go stateside I return with a few extra pounds so there's no doubt I miss certain foods, but those foods are also not good for me. I miss the technology and wish that our internet service was moving faster and I do wish we had better roads. When it rains a car can't drive up the clay road to our house at Promised Land and the road is just like pudding. I call it pudding hill until it's paved.

Access to mediums of entertainment is limited in Cape Coast and there are not as many social and cultural activities to get involved in, unless you're in Accra.

One can never get accustomed to poor sanitation practices and recycling is getting off to a slow start here.

Yes there are days when I get flustered feeling that nothing seems to work proper here in Ghana, at times it seems that lawlessness is increasing in society and laws are not enforced, when phone lines don't connect and I can't get on the web, or water runs out, the lights are shut off all in the same day, it's a bit much.

But all I have to do is look along the costal shore and see the slave dungeons in the distance to snap back to reality. The little agitating things I'm going through are nothing compared to what my ancestors endured. It helps me keep life in perspective. Otherwise for these few things I'm happy with my decision to live in my chosen homeland Ghana.

I've been asked how I've changed since coming to Ghana and the question caused me to pause to re-evaluate. I know I'm more tolerant of many things, differences, shortcomings, etc. I'm more patient and I hate to say it out loud because the universe has a way of bringing more things in my life to be patient about.

I pray I'm less judge-mental but I don't know if this is due to my being in Ghana or it's because I've been working on me and I hope I would have engaged in this work no matter where I found myself. I am less stressed and calmer and don't rush to do anything. I am more giving and forgiving, and learning not to sweat the small stuff.

I'm happier, enjoy my life, and I know the change of environment is the reason. I never want to see a winter season again. I wake up and go to sleep to the ocean waves and cool breeze. I know that I'm more courageous and confident. When I returned to the states last year I went to the mall with my sister-in-law Faye Clarke my first hubby's sister. She was amazed at how I sat still and watched the busyness going on all around me and how I was fully cognizant of everything that was going on around me. She said I appeared so calm and out of place from the crowd, and said if Ghana did that for me then she's planning her trip soon.

My life has truly been an adventure in Ghana, everyday there are new vistas to climb, new challenges to face, and life is never dull. I agree with Maya Angelo that yes, *"All God's Children Need Traveling Shoes"* also like she said I *"Wouldn't take Nothing for My Journey Now"*

I like to travel and last year I visited seven states in six weeks from the east coast to the west coast. I called it my "On My Own Tour" (Copying Pattie LaBelle). My next tour will be "I'm coming out!" Traveling is a good way to get to know yourself, especially when you travel alone and I am anxious to travel and see some new places. I even have to see Ghana's tourist sites. Kofi was so focused on finishing his work and it was hard to get him to stop and take a break. I haven't been to the Kwame Nkrumah

Memorial, neither the W.E.B. Du Bois Center. We did not sightsee and when we traveled it was usually for immigration purposes only. Also Kofi wouldn't have me travel around Ghana without him. So I'll be putting on my travelling shoes and coming to a city near you real soon.

I am not mad at America. I just wanted to come home. I have the best of two worlds. I'm an Afrikan Queen happy to have an American passport and a Ghanaian Green Card. I have a legacy in America, I'm not ashamed that my people helped to build that great country with free labor and I've reclaimed my legacy on the Continent of Afrika. I'm living in the proverbial Garden of Eden, eating from the tree of life and all is well. I am satisfied just to have my feet planted on the continent of Afrika, squeezing my toes in the sand. It is enough for me. I'm home.

Most of all I am a Child of God abounding in this great universe of unlimited possibilities, in this present moment, after moment, journey through timeless eternity. I love it! As I continue this excursion called life it now becomes one of self discovery, of honoring and celebrating myself, and learning to take better care of Adjoa. Relearning who is Adjoa without Kofi? What are my strengths, weaknesses, likes', dislikes and desires'? I'm happy to be alive. I'm just learning to be.

I know that God is consciousness. God is my life. God is my breath.

I have all my life heard a still small voice leading me in the right path. I have not always obeyed this voice but when I do obey it's always in my best interest. Countless times in my life I've heard a voice say go this way, not that way and later saw a calamity that I avoided by following that inner voice.

Since living in Ghana I recognize this voice as the Almighty, Most High, Alpha-Omega, The Only One True Living God, Omnipotent, Omniscient, Creator, Supreme Being, The One in Whom Everything and Everyone consists, The Originator, Onyame the Afrikans' Holy Ghost from time immemorial, The Spirit within me and not apart from me, and I walk on Holy Ground. This is my truth.

Life is bliss. We receive what we focus on. We only have to dare to dream and follow our hearts' desire. "Don't you know it is the Fathers' good pleasure to give you the kingdom? The Kingdom of God is within you, said the Lord."

My favorite chapter in the Bible is Romans chapter eight and I find it hard to pick a favorite verse; but I'll end with this one" What shall we say then to these things? If God is for us who can be against us? He who did not spare his own Son but gave him up for us all, how will he not also with him freely give us all things?"

Heaven is here in this moment and we experience it to the point that we as individuals can perceive it. Consciously take the journey . . . walk, run, fly, soar! Be. Enjoy the trip!

The author is available for discussion
groups and book parties by contacting:
takemehometoafrika@gmail.com.

Also see author featured in documentary:—An American Quest
for Authenticity by Cindy Ball. http://www.youtube.com/
watch?y=8jcUgutxlfg

Take Me Home to Afrika

The author is an advocate for the Akoma International Academy for Arts and Sciences in Ayensudo, Elmina in Ghana. This location is in one of the poorest regions of the country where education is most needed.

They need support from all quarters to keep their doors open in order to teach rural children whose parents cannot afford to pay for their education. These children will not be educated unless people who care about "minds being a terrible thing to waste" lend assistance.

Here is the Wish List for the school as of June 2011.

1. Paying students or scholarships for those who cannot pay.
2. New vehicle to transport students
3. Library setup
4. Librarian
5. Money
6. Playground equipment
7. Story books with people of color.
8. Projector for laptop
9. New computers
10. Manila file folders
11. Science furniture and fixtures
12. Science curriculum developer
13. Science instructor-primary level
14. Science experiment kits
15. Art supplies of all kinds
16. Music teacher
17. Music teacher-primary level for theory and practice

I encourage anyone who can help fulfill any of these items in cash or in kind, I thank you in advance for helping these youngsters expand their minds and for changing their lives for the better.

A luta Continua!

Mama Chekesha, PO BOX, 0114 UCC, CAPE COAST, GHANA www. akomainternationalacademy.com, 011-233-244105265

RECEIPT FOR DONATION TO AKOMA INTERNATIONAL ACADEMY FOR ART & SCIENCES

FROM: FOR AMOUNT: DATE

RECEIPT FOR DONATION TO AKOMA INTERNATIONAL ACADEMY FOR ART & SCIENCES

FROM: FOR AMOUNT: DATE

Mr. Willie Joe and Mrs. Ruth Merritt - My Parents

Sylvia (late) Joann Valerie Renee

The Merritt Sisters

Adjoa and son Latif

The Merritt clan in Philadelphia

Lee J and Netfa Harold

Angel Ann Our Earth Angel

Mr. & Mrs. Isaac and Anastasia Hooper

Our Wedding Picture

01/04/2011 18:49

Cape Coast Castle

Elmina Castle

Kofi playing his jazz drums

Kofi and unfinished house in Brenu

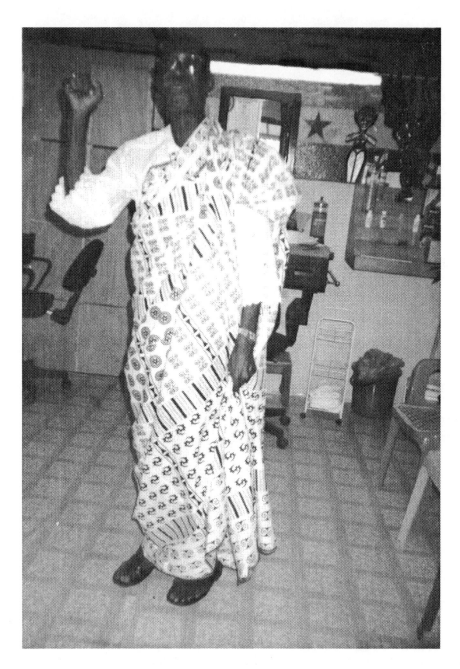

Kofi in his traditinal cloth.

Esteem Guesthouse

Kofi surveying Promise Land

Big Paa Kofi and Little Papa his namesake

Kofi and Adjoa at Obama party

Kofi and Adjoa's last birthday party together.

Nana Queen Esther Malkia Brantuo

Tony and Latif viewing Abanyie ancestral chart,

Willingboro N.J.

Abanyie family 2010

Latif on Stool, Abanyie family, Nana Afrakoh

and his linguist

Kofi Happy Building

Kofi's gravesite

Pa Kofi